SERVANT OF THE SERVICES

Central Support Unit
Catherine Street Dumfries DG1 1JB
tel: 01387 253820 fax: 01387 260294
e-mail: libs&i@dumgal.gov.uk

UK
CUSTOMER SERVICE EXCELLENCE
The Government Standard

Dumfries and Galloway
LIBRARIES
Information and Archives

24 HOUR LOAN RENEWAL ON OUR WEBSITE - WWW.DUMGAL.GOV.UK/LIA

SERVANT OF THE SERVICES

Jessie Howard

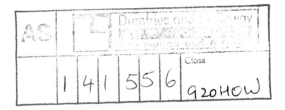
Book Guild Publishing
Sussex, England

First published in Great Britain in 2009 by
The Book Guild
Pavilion View
19 New Road
Brighton, BN1 1UF

Typesetting in Baskerville by
Keyboard Services, Luton, Bedfordshire

Printed in Great Britain by
CPI Antony Rowe

A catalogue record for this book is available from
The British Library

ISBN 978 1 84624 336 3

Contents

1

A Stroke of Luck

A brass band was practising Christmas carols in the Salvation Army building, but Jessie was too despondent to be cheered by the vibrant chords as she hurried towards the entrance to Carlisle Castle. At the wide-open gates, she glanced up at the formidable fortress, now the home of the Border Regiment: a squad of soldiers had emerged from the central archway and was marching down the roadway towards her. Turning left on to the gravel path, she automatically quickened her pace to keep ahead of the recruits, who were on their way to the hut next door to the cookhouse.

There were several entrances to the married quarters, an austere building along the perimeter of the Castle grounds, but the staircase leading to flat number 9 was easily found: opposite to the Naafi.

Preoccupied by her thoughts, Jessie climbed the stone steps and turned the handle to go into the flat, then closed the door again in consternation. Having checked the number, she re-opened the door to peer through the steam puffing upwards from a zinc bath, supported by two wooden chairs. The room now bore little resemblance to the neat scullery she had left three hours earlier. The coconut matting had disappeared; on the concrete floor there was now a pile of brown jackets and trousers, evidently awaiting their turn in the soapsuds. On the draining board, and submerged in clear water in the sink, there was even more brown canvas. The small wooden table, normally covered in brightly-coloured oilskin, was now littered with dozens of bachelor buttons. The only recognisable objects were father's pretty shaving cup and the brown case containing his open razor, which were kept out of harm's way on the high mantelshelf above the empty fire grate.

Mam came from the living room to turn off the tap. Her straight brown hair, usually swept up into a neat bun on the top of her head, now hung in damp wisps around her plump, red cheeks. 'Oh, there you are, Jessie. Did you get a job?' she asked expectantly.

'No, I didn't have any luck.'

'You've been an awful long time.'

'I went for a walk and found the church.'

Mam wiped her spectacles on her apron. 'I was sure they'd sent you after something.'

'A girl at the Labour Exchange said I wouldn't find a job in Carlisle.'

'Why not?'

'She asked me how old I am. I said I'm eighteen and she said I'm too old.'

'Too old?'

'She said the bosses take the lassies on at fourteen and put them off at eighteen, so they won't have to pay the extra insurance.'

'Was she the assistant?'

'No, she was signing on. And she said I'd have to wait six weeks before I get any dole money.'

'Och, she's making a mistake.'

'She said you can only draw the dole if you're stood off.'

'Didn't you explain to the assistant that you had to give in your notice at the glove factory when you couldn't find any lodgings?'

'Yes, but she just said to go back on Thursday.'

'Well then, stop worrying yourself.'

Jessie glanced at the washtub. 'I thought I'd come to the wrong flat when I opened the door.'

Mam's face lit up. 'I had such a stroke o' luck while you were out. Mrs Harris, upstairs, has bronchitis, poor soul, and I went up to help her. She's no' able to wash the canvas suits for the recruits, so I offered to help.'

'You'll never get them dried: it's real damp outside.'

'They'll dry on the pulley, .or on the rack round the fire.'

'They'll drip all over the place.'

'No, you haven't heard the best o' it. She's buying a new mangle and I can have the auld one for seven and six. We'll get it brought down tonight.'

'I've got ten shillings.'

'I'll get nine pence for every suit I wash, but if you lend me the money, you'll have it back as soon as I've finished this lot.'

'I'll give you a hand,' said Jessie, taking off her coat.

'No, we'll have a cup of tea, and if you wouldn't mind, the fire in the other room needs making up to keep the water hot.'

Mam picked up the blue vein soap and started to scrub the greasy collar of a jacket on the rubbing board. Jessie fetched the scuttle, followed by her sister Anna, who enquired if she had tried the biscuit factory or the 'sweetie place'.

'I thought I told you to keep an eye on Jamie,' said Mam.

'It's no' one eye yi need but two in the front and two in the back o' yir heed when he's around.'

'Don't you be so cheeky!' Mam waved the scrubbing brush at the retreating figure.

By the time Jessie had filled the scuttle in the scullery,

Jamie had removed the boot brushes from one of the footstools, which formed part of the fender in the living room. He was just about to prise open a tin of polish when Anna foiled his intentions. The two-year-old with the cherubic face and golden curly hair, stood with his hands behind his back, watching in disgust as she replaced the contents in the box. Then he looked down at his socks, darted over the hearthrug and slid across the brown polished lino. Jessie was surprised that he remained upright, but Anna was not impressed. 'He's usually trying to pull the aspidistra over his heed.'

Mary was sitting in the fireside armchair, concentrating on her knitting because she had dropped a stitch. Anna retrieved it and held up the inch wide strip. 'It's a scarf for Jamie.'

'That's lovely,' said Jessie.

Mary's heart-shaped face was solemn as her enquiring green eyes looked up. Having ascertained that Jessie was serious, she beamed with pleasure, revealing a wide gap between her top teeth.

Mam came from the scullery. 'Surely it's not too much to ask that one of you would mind the boy. It costs a fortune to keep him in socks.'

The outside door clicked. Father came through the scullery into the living room.

Mam looked at the clock. 'What brings you home so early, Jock?'

'I went to the canteen for a pint and got talking to the manageress. The Christmas party for the married families is tomorrow. She needs some help to wait at the tables, so I told her my auldest lassie is here. Would you like to help out for an afternoon Jessie?'

Mam quickly intervened. 'Of course you would. The manageress will explain what she wants done.'

'Well, if you think I'll be all right.'

'Of course you will,' said father. 'I'll go back and tell her straight away.'

Jessie wasn't entirely happy about her new job. However, she was slightly reassured when her stepfather promised to introduce her to the manageress: his sun-tanned complexion, red nose and waxed moustache gave him the air of a colonel; his ease of manner would smooth the introduction.

The following day, Father was waiting at the archway to accompany Jessie past the guard into the precincts, where there was a large cobbled square, bordered on two sides by tall modern buildings. He explained that these were the barracks: the castle itself was now used as a quartermaster's store. He chuckled as he pointed out that the English had managed to keep the Scots at bay for the past seven hundred years: they were only allowed to enter the castle as prisoners, to languish in the dungeons. Times had changed only slightly: although he was there by invitation, he too was confined to a dungeon, for that was where he worked. He was proud of his storeroom and started to tell Jessie about a stone, worn smooth by the tongues of prisoners because it gave off moisture. At any other time, she would have found all this very interesting, but now she just wanted to get the job done as quickly as possible. Mother's advice, to watch the other girls, sounded all right in theory, but she wasn't sure how it would work out in practice. How could she watch the other girls if she was supposed to be serving at table?

By now, they had reached a building on the left-hand side of the square. Jock pushed open the door of a room, furnished with green-topped tables and varnished chairs. A woman in her early thirties appeared behind the counter. 'Is this your daughter, Jock?'

'Aye, this is my lassie.'

'Good, thanks very much, Jock, I'll not forget you.' She turned to Jessie. 'Come through and I'll find you an overall.'

In a small room, Jessie removed her dress to put on a blue frock overall, cap and black tie. When she returned to the kitchen, the manageress locked the canteen; then accompanied her and two other assistants to the drill hall.

The next part was easy: it was simply a matter of laying the tables in preparation for a meal. Miss Price showed Jessie how to fold a serviette and commented that it didn't take her long to learn. Having inspected all the tables, she looked at the clock and suggested that they return to the canteen for a cup of tea, but it was not long before they were once again in the drill hall.

As they waited for the guests to arrive, the manageress started to allocate a section of the hall to each of her assistants, but her arrangement for the top table appeared to be the cause of some contention. Eventually, Jessie was assigned to a table at the far end of the hall and was relieved that the chairs were only along one side.

A group of bandsmen arrived and began to set up their music stands near the Christmas tree; it was not long before the guests began to arrive.

Having served her table, Jessie noticed that one of the other assistants was finding it difficult to keep up with the needs of the children, who were seated between the soldiers and their wives. She mopped up a drink and fetched a cloth to wipe some sticky fingers, then returned to her own table where the guests were less demanding.

Towards the end of the meal there was a lull: most of the people had finished eating and were either smoking or listening to the cheery music. The manageress had acted as overseer and was now standing near the door in conversation with a tall, slim man. Jessie felt slightly ill at ease because their glances in her direction gave the impression that they were discussing her.

The manageress beckoned to her. 'This gentleman is Mr Bird, the Area Supervisor. He wishes to speak to you.'

'Miss Edmondstone, I wonder if you would be interested in joining the Navy, Army and Air Force Institutes?'

Jessie didn't reply immediately: although she had managed to survive this particular ordeal, she knew that the Naafi canteen was meant for soldiers and was perturbed by the thought of serving in an all-male canteen.

Mr Bird continued, 'The pay is fifteen shillings a week, with full board and lodgings. You would have to leave home, of course, but there are splendid opportunities to travel. Some staff even go abroad.'

The offer sounded very reasonable. Jessie thought for a moment. 'Could I go home and discuss it with my mother? I'll come straight back and let you know.'

'Yes, do that. I'll be here for two hours.'

Jessie arrived home breathless, having run down the long drive.

The faint hope that Mam might veto the offer was quickly dispelled. 'I think you should take it. There's nothing here for you; girls born and bred in Carlisle can't find work, so there's not much chance for you, a stranger in the town.'

Jessie returned to the canteen to thank Mr Bird and receive further instructions. He issued her with a warrant, to be used on the railway, and gave directions about the journey to Bury in Lancashire. After a month's training she would then go to a place called Burscough.

In the evening, Father arrived home in good spirits: Jessie gathered that she had been a credit to him. The warrant officers had approved of the service they had received;

the other ranks had been amused, but very flattered, when she had made no distinction, addressing them all as 'sir'. There was some discussion as to where Burscough might be. As the family didn't possess an atlas, they had to rely on Father's knowledge that it was somewhere in the south of England.

Mam insisted that Jessie must go to bed early, but she lay awake, her brain teeming with the events of the day. When she had lit a candle in the church only the previous morning, she had not expected her prayer to be answered so soon. She surmised that Mam must now regret that in September she had left their rented house, and moved into a two-bedroom flat. When Jock had written to let her know that the post of barrack store man included accommodation, she had probably been anxious to join him in case he would have too much to drink and lose the job. It was obvious that Mam had been taken aback when Jessie had arrived on the doorstep on Christmas Eve. If only Mina's father hadn't come home unexpectedly and needed his bed, she could have remained in Aberdeen with her friend. She would also miss the social life at St Peter's, but Mr Bird had said that the Naafi liked to employ girls who go to church... The sound of voices interrupted her deliberations. Father was in a good humour, so Mam was taking the opportunity to obtain some pocket money for John and William. 'Thirty-five shillings is just no' enough to keep the bairns and send pocket money to the lads.'

'Well, you know, Mary lass, other people have to manage on their wages.'

'Could you not give me some of your pension?'

'I need a drink to drown my sorrows.'

'The war to end all wars was over ten years ago. You can't go on living in the past.'

'I fought and bled for ma pension.'

'Aye, you're right, Jock, you've bled nearly every beer barrel in the sergeant's mess.'

'You're aye on about Anna and her smart answers, but you've not got far to look, to see where she gets it from.'

'I'm only asking two shillings to send to John. I've not heard from him since he went to London.'

'He's not written because he's enjoying himself.'

'On boy's pay! It's more likely he canna' afford a stamp. If I'd had my way, they'd never have gone to the Queen Victoria.'

'Don't talk so daft, Mary, you should be pleased they're getting a good start in life. The training will stand them in good stead. It's every bit as good as the boarding schools the gentry send their sons to.'

'Aye, to train them to be officers.'

'He can rise through the ranks, and there'll be a good pension at the end.'

'But the parents send their sons some pocket money.'

'I'll have to think about it, Mary lass.'

'Well, don't think for too long, or we'll all be dead and buried.'

Jessie covered her head to shut out the voices. In Aberdeen, Mam had relied on her wages to help to pay the household expenses and send pocket money to John and William: sixpence, dipped in condensed milk to hold it firmly in the fold of the letter. John was now on boy service with the Scots Guards. His meagre pay would be spent on toiletries and cleaning equipment; there would be little to spare for any other expenses. Father now gave Mam all his wages but thought he was entitled to keep the pension he received for serving twenty-one years in the army. She didn't object to him spending most evenings in the convivial company of the sergeant's mess, but was aggrieved that he preferred to spend his pension on a round of drinks, rather than provide his own sons with pocket money.

Jessie knew that the argument would run its usual course: her mother would temporarily admit defeat. With a bit of luck, Father would still have some of his pension left in his pocket and, having celebrated Jessie's success, he would sleep soundly. There would be another argument when he discovered his half-crowns had changed into pennies overnight. Jessie was pleased that she would be making an early start: she would not be there to incriminate her mother. If father questioned her, he would regard her flushed cheeks as evidence of guilt.

Before they set off the next morning, Mam gave Jessie four half-crowns to repay the loan of the ten-shilling note. At the station she said, 'You'll be awful well off with fifteen shillings a week and nothing to pay out of it. You won't forget your poor old mother, will you?' She gave Jessie a hug and a kiss. 'Now don't go standing in any wee dark corners with those good-looking soldiers.'

Jessie boarded the train, but no sooner had she sat down than a thought occurred to her. At the carriage door she struggled to free the leather strap from the brass knob. The guard blew his whistle; the window dropped with a thud. 'Mam ... Mam...' A gush of steam drowned her parting words: 'I was supposed to go to the Labour Exchange and tell them I've got a job.'

2

First Encounter with the Sassenachs

A week had elapsed since Jessie's arrival at Bury, but she had suffered none of the pangs of homesickness that had beset her when she had been left behind in Aberdeen: she had been so busy that she had fallen asleep as soon as her head touched the pillow.

The daily routine began at seven a.m. when the general assistant, Gwyneth, and Jessie cleared the flues, black-leaded the range, filled the coal-scuttles, and lit the fire. While they were waiting for the kettle to boil, Gwyneth had first turn with the hand-basin in the bedroom, leaving Jessie to remove the fine layer of soot that had settled on the table and chairs in the kitchen.

By the time Gwyneth had taken morning tea to the manageress, the charge hand and cook had arrived for their early cup. Jessie used the delft with the Naafi crest from the kitchen dresser, but the staff each possessed a china cup and saucer, purchased at Woolworths: sixpence for a cup and three pence for a saucer.

The fire took a while to kindle, so cook would go into the pantry to write a list of the ingredients she required, while the charge hand wrote out the orders for the coffee bar. If the fire obliged, breakfast for the staff was at eight-thirty; a tray was taken up for the manageress, whose position of authority entitled her to this privilege.

After the breakfast washing up, the next task was to

clear the grates and re-lay the fires in the staff quarters. Apart from sweeping the bedroom floors and brushing the mats in the yard, the daily routine also included dusting and polishing the furniture. Gwyneth and Jessie didn't make the beds for the rest of the staff and their own were invariably spread up quickly to give the impression that they had been made.

Every day, the kitchen floor had to be scrubbed, half at a time; newspapers were used to protect the wet surface from dirty feet. It was also Jessie's job to prepare the vegetables on the draining board of the large white butler sink in the scullery, and to weigh up the ingredients for cook.

Lunch, at twelve-thirty, was followed by another round of washing up. The kitchen table was scrubbed every day, but the dresser, the cupboards underneath and the shelves in the pantry were cleaned in rotation.

Free time consisted of three hours every afternoon, and a half-day once a week. Jessie sometimes wrote a letter home, occasionally walked to the shopping centre at Bury, or made use of the time to do her washing.

Staff tea was a leisurely affair. Although the coffee bar opened at five-thirty, the trade of snacks and sandwiches rarely built up until later in the evening. Gwyneth and Jessie assisted cook, or helped the charge hand if she ran short of sandwiches.

The day ended officially at nine-thirty, but all the dishes and cooking utensils had to be washed up and put away before the staff drank their cocoa and retired for the night.

When Jessie first arrived at the barracks, she took an immediate liking to Mrs Hadley, the manageress, who had a pleasant expression and soft Irish accent. Although she was in her early thirties, she had overall responsibility for the canteen and grocery. Throughout the day she flitted in and out of the kitchen, her trim figure covered with an overall, which was dazzlingly white against her black stockings and shiny black shoes. On weekdays she was in the grocery bar, weighing up rations for the cookhouse, and serving the families who lived in the married quarters. She was free on Saturday afternoons and all day Sunday, but her duties included bookkeeping, which occupied a great deal of her spare time.

In comparison with the manageress, who was strict but had a kindly nature, the charge hand was abrupt and showed little patience when Jessie found it difficult to understand her Wigan accent. She had a habit of running one word into another and often referred to toll man. Jessie couldn't understand why tolls were collected in a barracks and asked cook, who was also puzzled. It was not until she repeated the word in context that cook laughed and explained that t'ol' man was the old man, in other words, the butcher.

Cook was a buxom Lancashire woman in her mid-thirties. Her plump face gave the impression that she was placid by nature, but she was often short-tempered due to pressure of work. Apart from preparing meals for the staff, she was responsible for the supper trade and made a variety of cakes and pastries for the coffee bar: the outside bakery only supplied the Naafi canteen with bread. Cook made it abundantly clear that she disliked having trainees foisted upon her because they got under her feet and, anyway, by the time she had explained what to do, she could have done the job three times over. She was forever complaining that Gwyneth had not pulled her weight since the arrival of the new assistant. However, Jessie was pleased to have a lively companion of her own age.

On her first night at the canteen, Jessie was surprised when she saw her roommate's artificial silk cami-knickers and crepe de chine nightdress. Her own pale blue fleecy-lined knickers and flannelette nightdress put her to shame: they were well worn and had begun to fade. When she admired the pretty lingerie, Gwyneth replied airily, 'My people are very comfortable. They have quite a large house in Wales.' She also boasted that she didn't have to work, but it was so dull being at home with nothing to do. She was engaged to a sergeant in the Lancashire Fusiliers and if he was also off duty, she returned late for tea, much to cook's annoyance.

Jessie was especially pleased when Gwyneth suggested that they walk to the shops after dinner, until she added that this would be a convenient arrangement since they would both be on duty in the coffee bar in the evening.

After lunch, they tidied the kitchen, as best they could, but they couldn't scrub the table because cook was still busy. After a while, she was fed up with them hanging around and dismissed them with a wave of her hand. 'Away you go, the pair of you. I'll do the rest.'

'Are you sure?' Jessie enquired, but Gwyneth didn't wait to hear the answer, she was already on her way to the bedroom and soon returned, wearing her coat over her overall. Jessie fetched her coat; then popped her head round the kitchen door to say, 'Goodbye'. There was a rich smell of spice as cook removed a baking tray from the oven. 'That smells lovely. What is it?'

'That's Nelson cake.' Cook anticipated her next question. 'It's a kind of bread pudding mixture, baked with pastry top and bottom. It uses up all the stale bread and the lads really enjoy a slice.'

Having satisfied her curiosity, Jessie caught up with Gwyneth, who had gone on ahead.

The weather was cold, so they walked briskly to the

shopping centre. Jessie bought two pairs of black stockings, at sixpence per pair, and a piece of elastic to make some new garters. However, they didn't stay long to look in the shop windows because it began to drizzle.

Back in the kitchen, cook had finished, so they sat round the fire and chatted until it was time to lay the table for tea. Gwyneth went upstairs and returned, a few minutes later, wearing her tie and cap. She looked prettier than usual, with her wavy hair fluffed up over her forehead and her face discreetly made up. 'I'll finish the table while you get ready,' she said. She seemed to have an uncanny knack of arriving just as a task had been completed.

In the bedroom, Jessie made sure that her plaits were still neatly in position across the back of her neck, and the badge on her cap was central; then hurried down to tea. On the stairs she passed Gwyneth, taking a tray up to Mrs Hadley's room. When she returned, a few minutes later, Jessie noticed that her bouffant hairstyle was now flattened.

After tea, Jessie was left to do the washing up. When she finally emerged from the scullery, Gwyneth was weighing up coffee on the kitchen scales, so she stood at the table to await instructions.

'The scale must be level: not one grain more, nor one grain less,' said Gwyneth, imitating Mrs Hadley. The knotted muslin was placed in a jug and covered with boiling water. Next, it was the turn of the cocoa and sugar; the pan descended with a bump. Gwyneth removed the cocoa until the scale was level, then took another spoonful of the powder off the pan and put it back in the tin. She looked at Jessie and laughed at her puzzled expression. 'That's one less for Gwyneth because she likes it weak,' she said in her singsong voice.

The staff usually drank the leftover cocoa when the bar closed. It cloyed to the palate because it had evaporated while it sat on the hob throughout the evening, but Jessie doubted if the slight variation in the recipe would make much difference. She enquired, 'How do you know how much cocoa to put in?'

'It's all in the book of rules,' said Gwyneth, pointing to the Naafi manual on the dresser. She continued to stir the cocoa and evaporated milk to a smooth paste before adding the boiling water. 'Now, for my next demonstration: a jug of tea.' She tore off the top of a paper packet of approximately 1½ ounces of tea; tipped the contents on a piece of white muslin and tied it with a knot. Having placed it in a white enamel jug, she added boiling water from the urn. 'You have to leave room for the sugar and evaporated milk. They go in after the tea is brewed, but mind you take the muslin out first though.'

'How many cups does that make?'

'Nineteen. The tea is very strong and you could make more if you put the bag in another little jug, but you're not allowed to.'

By now, the coffee had infused. Gwyneth removed the muslin bag with a large metal spoon and carried the jug into the bar. Jessie was left to tidy the kitchen, but she was pleased to do anything to postpone the next assignment.

The coffee bar was empty when Jessie rejoined Gwyneth a few minutes later.

'Now don't forget, you are Miss Edmondstone and I am Miss Jones.'

'Where are all the soldiers?

'It's always slack when the men have athletics. That's why the charge hand has Wednesday afternoon off.'

At that moment, the first arrivals came through the door.

'Two coops of char, looks like coffee, tastes like cocoa,' said the first man.

His companion glanced round the empty bar and leaned

on the counter, cupping his face in his hands. 'Which night am I taking you out?' The question was directed at Gwyneth.

'I'm very particular who I go out with,' said Gwyneth, as she placed the cups on the counter.

'How about it, miss?' The recruit shifted his gaze to Jessie.

Gwyneth didn't give her the chance to reply. 'It's no use asking her, she's leaving soon.'

The first soldier ordered the suppers. 'Bangers, peas and mash twice.'

When Gwyneth returned with the suppers, she said, 'That's one and tuppence. Miss Edmondstone will take the money.'

As they carried their tea to a table, the first soldier tipped the other one off. 'No chance there, Spud, she's engaged to a sergeant.'

A few recruits drifted into the room and sat down at the tables; then two more soldiers arrived. The first man asked, 'Is that tea stewed?'

Jessie glanced at Gwyneth, who replied, 'It's freshly brewed.'

'Freshly brewed half an hour ago,' commented his companion.

'All right, I'll believe you, thousands wouldn't. Two coops of char and two slices of mystery cake.'

· As Jessie poured the tea, she made a quick deduction: on the shelves in the cupboard under the stand there were wire trays of rock cakes, doughnuts and Nelson cake. The latter had been a mystery to her earlier, so she served up two slices and waited.

'How much is that?'

'Four pence please.' She had guessed correctly.

At nine twenty-five, the orderly corporal came into the coffee bar to call, 'Time'. All the customers stood up to leave, bidding the staff a cheery 'Goodnight'. Gwyneth closed the door and took the black cash-box into the kitchen, leaving Jessie to tip the tea leaves and coffee grounds out of the muslin bags into the bucket in the scullery. When she returned, she measured the leftover tea with a cup. 'Six cups,' she said, as she poured the last cup down the sink. 'You must remember to write the number in the book.'

The next job was to pour the coffee into a clean jug and put it in the pantry while Gwyneth went to the office to give the takings to Mrs Hadley.

By the end of the fourth week, Jessie was beginning to feel more at ease, and now had mixed feelings about going to Burscough. When Mr Bird arrived to arrange her transfer, he asked her how she was getting on.

'All right,' she replied and looked to Mrs Hadley for confirmation.

'You are quite happy with the job?'

'Yes,' she hesitated, then added, 'the only trouble is that the soldiers use slang and I can't understand them, especially if they talk with a cigarette in their mouth.'

Mr Bird was sympathetic. 'You will probably find it much easier at the Depot. Most of the men are artificers and tradesmen. They come from various parts of the country. Mrs Hadley's sister is the manageress. I'm sure she will help, as there will only be the two of you.'

3

Servitor Servientium

The exact location of Burscough remained a mystery throughout Jessie's apprenticeship at Bury, but the explicit instructions, issued by the supervisor, guided her on her journey to a small station on the outskirts of Ormskirk. The only passenger to alight from the train, she hurried along the wet platform towards the exit, where the ticket collector confirmed she was heading in the right direction. She tucked the brown paper parcel of her possessions inside the lapel of her gabardine, to protect it from the drizzle, and set off along the road leading out of the village. At first she made slow progress on the grassy verge, with the wet turf squelching under her feet, but when she found there was no traffic, she took to the tarmac to walk briskly into the rain-soaked countryside.

It seemed a long half-mile before Jessie came to an un-named track between the fields, but the sight of the earth, churned up by the tyres of heavy vehicles, convinced her that this must be 'the turning on the right' leading to the Depot. She picked her way across the puddles in the wheel tracks; then walked along the side of the lane to avoid the slippery mud. She was so intent on watching her step that she was unaware of a staked and wired fence until she came across a board, lying in the wet grass, which warned that trespassers would be prosecuted. Inside the enclosure, there was another board with Royal Army

Ordnance Corp. Depot written in large letters and nearby, a sentry box, which had sunk at an angle into the long grass.

Jessie walked through the open gateway, half expecting a guard to appear, but there was no one there to either challenge or direct her. The buildings ahead had no distinguishing features; neither did another cluster to the right, so she decided to shelter from the driving rain while she considered her next move. Having retrieved the parcel from inside her coat, and straightened the brim of her velour, she was just about to set forth when the sound of whistling heralded the arrival of a young man.

'Excuse me, please could you direct me to the Naafi canteen?' she requested, as she emerged from the sentry box.

The startled soldier came to an abrupt halt. The corners of his mouth twitched with amusement as he replied, 'Sure, I'm going in that direction. I'll show you the way.'

Jessie walked in step with the soldier, expecting him to enquire her business, but the rain was dripping off the peak of his cap and running in rivulets down his greasy boiler suit, so he looked straight ahead.

'I'm the new canteen girl.'

The remark was greeted with a low whistle from the soldier's pursed lips but, otherwise, the silence remained unbroken until they reached a grocery store with Naafi over the entrance. Finding the door locked, he gave a loud rat-a-tat on the clear glass pane. While they waited for an answer, Jessie stood on the step and could see through an open inner door into the adjoining room where a woman appeared to be scrubbing a table. The soldier gave a second rat-a-tat, but the woman seemed oblivious of their presence.

'Oh, I forgot, Saturday's early closing and she won't open on any account. I'll show you the back door.'

Jessie followed the young man round the end of the single-storey brick building, with windows above shoulder level, and curtains identical to those of the staff quarters at Bury.

The soldier lifted the latch on a painted door; then stood aside to allow Jessie to enter a back yard. Ducking under the clothesline, he conducted her past the open doors of a coal shed and a toilet, then rapped on a third door before entering.

The warmth that greeted them was emitted by a metal cylinder near a deep white butler sink, but in other respects the small scullery was similar to the one at Bury: there were no cupboards, and only a single shelf for the saucepans.

A sharp rap on the kitchen door brought an immediate response. The irate woman, who opened it, was dressed in similar fashion to Mrs Hadley: her white overall, open at the front, revealing a navy blue skirt and white blouse.

'How many times do I have to tell you? No serving after hours.'

'Thank you, all the same, but I don't need serving. I've brought your new assistant,' replied the young man, courteously, but with a tinge of relish, as he stepped aside and inclined his head towards Jessie.

The manageress was obviously taken aback, and Jessie was so surprised by the exchange that she was only vaguely aware of the soldier's parting words, 'Good luck with your new job, miss. Good afternoon.'

'You soon found yourself a boyfriend,' said the manageress, as she eyed her new assistant up and down.

For a moment, Jessie was nonplussed; then hastened to explain that there was nobody at the gate to direct her. The soldier had merely accompanied her because he happened to be coming that way. The manageress made no further comment and sat down at the table to read the letters from the supervisor and her sister, while Jessie remained standing.

Miss Taylor bore a faint resemblance to her sister, in that her eyes were blue and her skin slightly transparent, but her features were not so fine and her front teeth overlapped. At first sight, Jessie had presumed that she was younger than Mrs Hadley: her youthful figure, slender legs and trim ankles were deceptive. Under closer scrutiny, her shingled black hair was flecked with white, and there were crow's feet under the light dusting of powder on her face. The indications were that she was nearer to forty than thirty.

The manageress finished reading the letter from the supervisor and glanced at Jessie. 'I see you're a Catholic. It's going to be difficult for us both to get to Mass on Sunday. You'll have to go at eight; I go at eleven.' She opened the letter from her sister. 'Hang your coat and hat over the scullery door to dry ... the kettle's nearly boiling.'

Eventually, she made a pot of tea and pointed to the only other chair at the far end of the table. Jessie sat down and waited while she poured a Naafi cup, and a china cup for herself. By now the manageress had recovered her composure. 'I have my own china cup and saucer. It makes the tea taste so much nicer. You'll have to buy a cup for yourself.' From her pocket, she produced a packet of Capstan, which she proffered. Jessie refused politely, explaining that she didn't smoke.

'It's a bad habit and very difficult to break. I've tried, but it's best not to start.' She felt in her pocket for a box of matches. There was a pause as she puffed at the cigarette; then endeavoured to justify her treatment of the young man. 'I'm sick and tired of married families and soldiers who forget things. If they had their way, I'd never have any time off.' She continued to make polite conversation, enquiring about Mrs Hadley and the staff at Bury, with whom she appeared to be well acquainted. Having stubbed out her cigarette, she asked, 'Have you finished your tea? Come along and I'll show you round.'

The first stop was the grocery bar. Jessie was impressed with the cleanliness and neat arrangement: all the provisions were stacked on the shelves behind the counter, except for the potatoes, flour and sugar, which were in the three sacks on the floor. The manageress then conducted Jessie along a passage to a room furnished with a desk, a locker, a chest of drawers and two armchairs, one upholstered with leather, the other made of varnished wood. Jessie caught a glimpse of a bed behind a screen before the manageress drew her attention to the grate of the red-tiled fireplace. 'That will be one of your duties, to clean the grate and light the fire, and see it's kept alight during the day. I have been forced to keep the office floor clean myself,' she added in an aggrieved tone.

The next room along the passage was furnished with two single beds and a dressing table with a large mirror and four deep drawers. There was also a locker, a wooden chest and a cupboard with hooks for outdoor clothes.

'Doesn't it smell stale!' The manageress opened both windows in an effort to drive out the odour of perspiration and stale tobacco.

Although the room was a replica of the one Jessie had shared with Gwyneth at Bury, it compared very unfavourably: the grubby blankets lay folded on one of the beds; the washbasin in the corner had a greasy rim; the brown lino needed a scrub and the fawn mats in front of each bed were covered in fluff and feathers.

The manageress cast Jessie a sidelong glance, as if to assess her reaction. Instead of divulging her true feelings, Jessie quickly conjured up a comment that wouldn't give offence. 'The Naafi crest on the mats is rather nice. I'll soon have them brushed up.'

While the manageress was collecting the linen from a walk-in cupboard in the passage, Jessie discovered two feather eiderdowns under the faded blue cover on one of the single beds. She was transferring one to the other bed when the manageress returned.

'There you are, clean sheets, pillowcases, towel, two blue overalls, tie and cap. The overalls will have to do you for a week. There are some on order and they should arrive soon.' As she left the room she added, 'When you do the laundry list, include two of these blankets. They could do with a wash. Come to the kitchen when you've changed into your overall.'

Having sorted out the cleanest blankets to put on her bed, Jessie put on one of the overalls and made her way back to the kitchen, stopping at the end of the passage to take her bearings.

On her right was the door to the grocery and another door, which was bolted shut. Along the centre of the adjacent wall stood the kitchen dresser, with the entrance to the coffee bar to the right and the larder to the left. In front of the window, which overlooked a yard, there was a long wooden table: one end was near the door of the larder; the other end was opposite the range, which backed on to the scullery.

As she stood, looking around, Jessie had the impression that the kitchen had been hastily tidied in readiness for her arrival. She mused that it should not be too difficult to keep the red congoleum floor clean when all the scuffmarks were removed.

The manageress appeared. 'Come and see the coffee bar where you will be in charge. I've been cleaning the stand for you.'

Jessie followed her through the entrance into an elongated room, lit with an electric light. Beside the dividing wall there was an ornate stand, painted with white enamel.

24

The upper half was curved to accommodate the Naafi crest, painted in blue; the shelf, below it, stretched full width. The central mirror was too high to serve any useful purpose and on either side there were four small shelves, supported at the front with vertical rods of carved dowel. The lower half of the dresser consisted of a cupboard with three sliding doors. On top of the cupboard there was a bowl of water and a cloth.

'If you wash up, I'll finish the stand,' said the manageress.

Jessie stepped carefully over the glass pedestals and miscellaneous assortment of goods, strewn on the floor between the stand and the counter. When she reached the sink in the alcove, at the far end, she requested some scouring powder and soda. The soda was under the sink, but the scouring powder had evidently not been in much demand: the manageress had to fetch a jar.

Jessie began to scrub the sink, but found it very difficult to remove the dirt lodged in the pitted metal, which was probably an alloy of zinc. However, the dark mahogany draining board responded to washing and rinsing.

By the time she had finished washing all the glass dishes, the manageress had wiped the paint on the lower part of the stand and replaced most of the display. The heart-shaped wooden containers now held a colourful arrangement of apples and oranges; one glass-domed pedestal was filled with cakes; the other held a clean doiley in readiness for the cheese sandwiches. As she propped up two boxes, each containing three-dozen bars of chocolate, the manageress commented, 'Duncan's hazelnut is very popular and they're only a penny; Cadbury's are two pence and they're just plain milk.'

Jessie had gradually become aware of a clicking noise behind the shuttered counter. The manageress explained that the men were playing billiards in the mess. 'They prefer that room because there's a piano and a gramophone, and also a good fire, but the beer bar's over there.' She pointed to the other end of the counter.

Jessie followed her to a small annexe, where there were two beer barrels and several crates of beer and lemonade. The manageress opened a serving hatch to show her a small dark room with an exit at the opposite end. There was also another door, which appeared to be the reverse side of the bolted door in the kitchen.

'It's very gloomy. You can see why the men prefer to stay in the mess.'

Having closed and bolted the hatch, she enquired, 'Do you know anything about beer?'

'No, there was no beer at Bury.'

'Oh well, I suppose you'll learn!'

When the coffee bar was tidy, they returned to the kitchen for a meal of ham and tomatoes, followed by tinned peaches and evaporated milk.

After tea, the manageress remained seated at the table, to enjoy her cigarette, and Jessie was instructed to transfer the dishes to the scullery. While she was washing up at the sink, she looked out of the window and could see through the glazed door of a building on the opposite side of the yard, where two men in white were drinking from large mugs.

Back in the kitchen, the larger window provided a clearer view.

'What's that place over there?'

'The men's cookhouse, Corporal Smythe is in charge, and a word of warning, begin as you mean to go on! No credit, no lending money, no back-door trade, and no Christian names. It doesn't pay to be too familiar with the troops.'

The lecture over, Jessie was sent to fill the three coal-scuttles and light the fire in the office. She expected that her next duty would be to prepare the drinks for the coffee bar, but when she returned to the kitchen, she was surprised to find the table now covered with roasting tins containing liver and onions, sausages, and four pork chops.

'I'll tell you what to do tonight but this is really your job,' said the manageress.

Although Jessie had assisted the cook at Bury, she was completely unprepared for her new catering duties.

'Weigh up three pounds of potatoes: that will make nine portions. You'll have to be quick. The peas are already soaked but you'll have to hurry if the vegetables are to be ready for the supper trade.'

By the time Jessie had peeled the potatoes, the tins had been transferred from the table to the oven. If this was to be her new job, past experience had taught her that she couldn't afford to miss an opportunity to find out what to do. 'How do you get the oven the right heat?'

The manageress was chalking the menu on a board. 'You have to put the right amount of coal on the fire. Make sure the flues are well raked out when you clean the range in the morning.'

A loud banging came from the direction of the coffee bar.

'Take no notice. That will be Lance Corporal Craig, looking for his pint. Change your overall as quickly as you can.'

There was no time to re-plait her hair, but Jessie made sure her uniform was correct before she returned to the bar, where the manageress was taking down the shutters.

'This should have been my half day, but I had to postpone it.'

Jessie wasn't sure if she was expected to apologise for the inconvenience but, by then, the last shutter had been removed, revealing a solitary soldier with his elbow leaning on the counter.

'A pint of bitter please.' The lance corporal, with a

long service stripe on his sleeve, was watching two soldiers playing billiards at the far end of the room. He gave his order without so much as a glance in their direction.

'Corporal Craig, this is our new assistant, Miss Edmondstone,' said the manageress, with some hesitation.

The lance corporal with sandy coloured hair, greying at the temples, turned slowly. Jessie couldn't help noticing the depth of the two vertical furrows at the middle of his brow as he studied her with penetrating eyes. His chest expanded as he straightened himself up to his full five feet ten, and inspected her as if she were on parade. 'Do you know the meaning of the motto on your cap?'

Jessie shook her head in bewilderment.

'Well, I'll tell you then. Servitor Servientium is Latin. It means servant of the services. The Naafi has a monopoly and we are obliged to deal with them, but just take note.' He brought his fist down firmly on the counter. 'Service we mean to have! We don't want greasy cups; neither do we like cigarette ash floating in our tea; forks should not have yesterday's meal between the prongs; beer should be sparkling and clear, not like dishwater; a pint should be a pint, and not half froth. I don't expect to stand here and wait while you indulge in a tête à tête...'

As the tirade continued, Jessie detected the faintest trace of a Scottish accent. At first she had been disconcerted by the vehemence of the unexpected attack, but now she was filled with indignation: it was unthinkable that the first Scotsman she had encountered in England should address her in this fashion. She waited until he had discharged his pent-up wrath. Then, although her knees were trembling, she said boldly, 'Would it no' be fairer t' see whit I can dae before yi start on me?'

The lance corporal's vehemence turned to astonishment. 'Well, I'll be damned. By all that's wonderful, a Scot! Where do you come from?'

Reassured by the complete change in his manner, Jessie replied, 'The land of clever lads and bonnie lassies.'

'And which part might that be?'

'Ayrshire.'

'Ayrshire, I know it well, Rabbie Burns country where they breed poets and the best cattle in the world. How did you come to be in Burscough?'

'My father did twenty-one years in the Gordons. When he was discharged, he became storekeeper at Carlisle Castle. He got me this job.'

The lance corporal held out his hand. 'Put it here miss. If anyone in this depot says a word out of place, Jock Craig will sort it out.'

Miss Taylor had meanwhile been polishing a glass until it shone like crystal. 'Miss Edmondstone, come and I'll show you how to draw a pint.'

Jessie watched as the glass was placed under the tap, lowered and then raised, to ensure that it contained the correct quantity of beer with a layer of froth on top.

'Is that all right for you corporal?'

'Yes, thank you, that will do fine.'

The lance corporal smiled and nodded as Jessie followed Miss Taylor back to the kitchen.

As soon as she was out of earshot, the manageress said, 'That man is the bane of all the Naafi girls. You seem to have found favour for the time being, but just watch your step. Lance Corporal Craig doesn't complain to me, he goes straight to the supervisor.'

There was a knock on the bar counter. 'Service please.'

'Hello, where did you come from?' asked the next customer.

'This is Miss Edmondstone, all the way from bonnie Scotland,' said the lance corporal.

'That will please you, Jock. Could you rustle me up a

couple of ham sandwiches?' The question was directed at Jessie.

'I'll find out.'

In the kitchen the manageress frowned, 'Just a minute.' She peered through the entrance at the private. 'Tell him there are no ham sandwiches, but the cheese are freshly made.'

When Jessie expressed her regrets, the young man settled for cheese without demur.

Although the manageress appeared to be completely absorbed in her accounts, Jessie had the feeling that she was strategically positioned at the kitchen table to deal with any emergency. She came into the bar, occasionally, on some pretext. 'Don't forget to fill the sink with hot water before you put the cups in; they'll break if you run the tap on them.'

Jessie had been well trained in the art of washing up but she appreciated any advice. 'Yes, thank you, Miss Taylor,' she replied.

When the supper trade began at seven o'clock, Jessie went into the kitchen to place the orders. The manageress made it clear that the suppers were the responsibility of the general assistant, but she supervised to make sure the portions were correct.

Each time Jessie went to fetch a supper, her presence seemed to distract the manageress, even if she didn't speak.

'It's the very devil to make the nett and surplus balance.'

'What's the nett?' Jessie enquired, in case this was another duty she was about to acquire.

'The tea and sugar are the nett, but when they are sold, they become the surplus,' she replied irritably.

Jessie was none the wiser. To her relief, the manageress added, 'You'll have to do this one day. I don't suppose you'll be a general assistant all your life.'

'No,' said Jessie, thankfully: this was one problem that could be shelved.

The conversation was interrupted by a knock on the back door: a tall, dark-haired soldier came through the scullery.

'Good evening, Sergeant Brown. Meet my new assistant, Miss Edmondstone to the men, but Jessie off duty.'

'How are you getting on?' enquired the sergeant as he shook Jessie's hastily wiped, but still greasy, hand. She was slightly disconcerted because his slender hands were so clean. However, she felt more at ease as she looked up at his pleasant smile.

The manageress answered on Jessie's behalf. 'Very well, apart from the fact that she asks me something every time I'm halfway up a column of figures.'

'Give me the books, Molly. I'll take them to the office.'

'Thank you, Cyril. Is my fire all right, Jessie?'

Jessie refuelled the fire then returned to find the manageress and the sergeant deep in conversation. She had already noticed the ring on the third finger of Miss Taylor's left hand, so she discreetly made herself scarce.

In the coffee bar the lance corporal was still leaning on his elbow at the end of the counter, but there were no customers. Jessie stood in the alcove and used a nailbrush to clean the handles of the cups, which were stained with tannin.

The manageress startled her by peering over her shoulder. 'You can't stay here all night. You're supposed to be looking after the suppers.'

Back in the kitchen, there was just time to cover the containers, to prevent the food from drying out in the oven, before she was summoned by a rat-a-tat on the counter.

'Have you anything else apart from that?' The corporal nodded in the direction of the menu board.

'No, I'm sorry, we haven't.'

'Give me a couple of ham sandwiches.'

'I'm sorry, we've no ham.'

When the corporal started to remonstrate, the manageress quickly appeared on the scene. 'Good evening, Corporal Skinner, can I get you anything? How about bacon, eggs, tomatoes, bread and butter and a cup of coffee?'

As these items were not on the menu, Jessie couldn't make up her mind if they were subject to availability, or if the manageress had just forgotten them.

A few minutes later, Miss Taylor presented the corporal with a supper, cooked to perfection and tastefully presented. It was not surprising that the next three customers also decided that the meal looked appetising. Having passed the orders to Jessie, the manageress joined the sergeant in the office.

The bacon was soon sizzling in the pan but the eggs posed a problem. The knife sliced straight through the shell, causing the yolk to mingle with the white as it plopped out of the cup.

Three failures later, Jessie knocked on the office door. 'Miss Taylor, could you help me please?'

The manageress broke three more eggs into cups and advised Jessie to camouflage the broken ones by covering them with hers. Jessie's culinary efforts compared very unfavourably with those of her superior, but the soldiers accepted their suppers without comment.

Although Jock Craig only drank two pints throughout the entire evening, he continued to prop up the bar. He was a regular customer and well versed in the procedure. Jessie had only to hesitate and he came to the rescue, directing her to the correct cupboard or drawer, or explaining what her predecessor would have done in similar circumstances. She was grateful for his assistance and thanked him when he bade her 'Goodnight' at closing time.

The second shutter was already in position when a breathless civilian dashed into the bar. 'Could I have a cup of tea and a couple of sandwiches, miss?' He requested the favour in a soft Irish brogue.

'You can have the sandwiches but the tea is finished.'

'A cup of cocoa,' he persisted.

Jessie was about to pour the cocoa from the jug on the stove when Miss Taylor appeared. 'Surely you're not serving cocoa at this time of night. You're supposed to be closed.' She marched into the bar to reprimand the real culprit. 'I might have known it was you, Private Riley. You know perfectly well we close at half past nine.'

'Sure now, your clock is always fast.'

The manageress turned to Jessie. 'When that clock says nine-thirty, there's no more serving. There must be no exceptions.'

'It was only ten past nine on the station clock.'

'Well, that will teach you not to drag your feet.'

'You expect me to run here at the double, to be in time for your early closing.'

'I suppose it wouldn't suit your convenience to catch an earlier train.'

He ignored the sarcastic remark and transferred his attention to Jessie. 'I like your new assistant.'

'Less of the blarney! She may be new but that doesn't mean you can take advantage.'

'I'm doing you a favour, eating up these sandwiches. They're so dry they're curling up at the edges. All I'm asking is a drink to wash them down.'

'Nonsense, they don't dry out under the glass!'

He changed his tactics. 'I just don't know how you could be sleeping in your bed tonight, knowing that you refused to serve a fellow countryman on the point of starvation.'

The manageress relented: 'Miss Edmondstone, give

33

Private Riley a cup of cocoa, but make sure this is the first and last time he's served after hours.'

Having kept a straight face throughout the battle of wits, Jessie managed to hide her amusement as she served the victor with a cup of cocoa.

Completely unrepentant, the handsome Irishman, with deep blue eyes and brown curly hair, gave her a roguish wink as she put up the last shutter.

Jessie counted the takings and left ten shillings in the float. Miss Taylor made a tour of inspection, closing the lids of chocolate boxes tightly before she placed them in the drawers. Having satisfied herself that everything was in order, she helped to put away the kitchen utensils, then placed a cloth on the table. While Jessie was finishing the washing up, she made cocoa for three and called 'Cyril' for his supper.

As the ham sandwiches were passed round, the sergeant asked Jessie how she had managed on her first evening. Before she had time to reply, Miss Taylor said, 'Mrs Hadley said in her letter that Jessie was nervous about going into the bar, so I went in to introduce her. It was a good job I did because Craig was in one of his moods and gave her a lecture, the cheek of the fellow.'

Sergeant Brown gave Jessie the benefit of his advice: 'You don't want to take too much notice of the lance corporal. He's the self-appointed spokesman and custodian of the lower ranks.'

'Barrack room lawyer, you mean.' There was a sharp edge to her voice as Miss Taylor put her own interpretation on his words.

'No, he's quite a decent chap, really. He joined the army when he was young and discipline was strict. As a result, he has no time for inefficiency.'

'He was all right to me afterwards.'

'Oh, she really trounced him.' There was more than a hint of satisfaction in Miss Taylor's voice.

34

At that moment, a tabby cat came stealthily from the direction of the passage; the manageress noticed him immediately. 'That cat's been in the bedrooms again. It's Florrie's fault for encouraging him. You must remember to keep the doors shut, Jessie.'

'I don't know why you keep him,' said the sergeant.

'He's supposed to be a good mouser, but there was a hole gnawed in the sugar sack this morning.'

'They feed him too well in the cookhouse. You'd be better off with a few mouse traps.'

The polite conversation continued. Jessie had heard the expression 'two's company', so she gulped down her cocoa and, explaining that she hadn't unpacked, retired to her room.

The parcel containing her few belongings lay on the bedroom floor, where she had deposited it earlier in the day. The brown paper had completely disintegrated and her clothes were damp, despite the fact that the wind was whistling round the room. She closed the windows and pulled the heavy, lined cretonne curtains to shut out the cold blast; then untied the string and shook the damp garments to flatten them. She looked for the stone hot water bottle the manageress had promised her when she arrived. The locker only contained a chamber pot, which appeared to be empty, but the smell was so obnoxious that she quickly closed the cupboard door. She felt her nightdress again: it was slightly damp and very cold. If the sergeant had departed, she could ask permission to air her nightdress at the kitchen range, but if he were still in the kitchen, she would just ask for a hot water bottle.

There was no sound as Jessie walked along the passage, but when she reached the door, there were voices in the direction of the scullery.

'Mrs Hadley said in her letter she's a quiet, rather timid

girl. I was quite taken aback when she trounced Craig. Mind you, he needs to be put in his place. He's always complaining.'

'You must admit, Molly, not without some justification.'

'Well, what can I do? I have to accept anyone the Naafi cares to send.'

Jessie lingered, on the assumption that the sergeant would retire to his bunkhouse at any moment, but the conversation continued.

Back in her room, she shivered as she took off her overall and climbed into bed, still wearing her underclothes.

4

Keeping the Sabbath Day Holy

On Sunday morning Jessie awoke with the noise of the soldiers on fatigues in the sergeant's mess. When she switched on the light, the alarm clock on the chest of drawers said quarter past six. Although her duties didn't begin until seven, she decided to get up because Miss Taylor had promised to accompany her to Mass at eight o'clock.

Apart from a shaft of light from the cookhouse, the kitchen was in darkness, but it was instantly illuminated by the flick of a switch. Jessie mused that the electric light was much better than gas, which had to be so carefully ignited: the slightest vibration caused the fragile mantle to disintegrate.

The range was soon raked out; the paper and wood kindled to a bright blaze. Jessie was about to empty the ash box, but changed her mind: it would be better to put the kettle on first. As she crossed the scullery to reach the light switch, there was a crunching noise under her feet. She turned to fill the kettle and was horrified to find the floor covered in black beetles, scurrying in all directions; the bottom of the sink was also a writhing mass of black.

After the initial shock, she pulled herself together and tried to decide what to do. The beetles were too large to go down the drain and if she ran the tap, they would clog the plughole. She was still considering how she would remove them, when Miss Taylor appeared in her dressing gown and curling pins. 'Haven't you got the kettle on yet?'

'The sink is full of beetles.'

'They're not beetles, they're cockroaches, but that doesn't prevent you filling the kettle. Remember to use cold water.'

Jessie stepped towards the sink, transfixed by the sight of the cockroaches, crawling up the slippery sides. By now, several of them had fallen on their backs and lay helplessly with their legs waving in the air.

The manageress snatched the kettle. 'You can't stand there all day.'

Having recovered sufficiently to remove the centre ring of the hob, Jessie asked, 'Where did all they things come from?'

The manageress placed the kettle over the flame. 'If you mean the cockroaches, they always come where there's warm, damp heat.'

'But how am I going to get rid of them?'

'One of the men on fatigues will remove them when he comes for a bucket of water. You can give him five Woodbines. Now don't waste any more time. Bring a cup of tea to my room when you've made it.'

The soldier duly arrived and responded cheerfully to the request: 'Certainly, have you got a shovel handy?'

Bang, bang, bang, the cockroaches cracked and squelched as he set about them, using the shovel as a weapon. After two journeys to the back door, he ran the taps at full volume. Jessie thanked him, profusely, as she handed over the cigarettes.

'Any time, miss,' he said, and went whistling on his way.

Despite the extra quarter of an hour, it was a rush to get ready for Mass, but on their return, Miss Taylor made up for lost time by helping to prepare breakfast.

The manageress was officially off duty all day Sunday, but the general assistant was only free for three hours in the afternoon. Sunday morning duties were light: apart from the usual round of washing up, there were only the sandwiches for the bar, and vegetables to prepare for dinner. Promptly, at twelve o'clock, Jessie removed the shutters and was surprised to find the customers immaculate in their uniforms. She gathered from the ensuing conversation that they had been on church parade.

The six rounds of sandwiches soon disappeared; Jessie quickly made another six. Every customer wanted sandwiches with tea or coffee and the situation was gradually getting out of hand. She worked frantically on the next pile of sandwiches, only to find that the tea and coffee had nearly run out. The men were patient and courteous, but she became increasingly flustered. Finally, in desperation, she went to find the manageress.

Miss Taylor came to the rescue by making more tea, but her displeasure was obvious. She soon returned to weighing up commodities in the grocery bar.

When the rush was over, Jessie's relief was short lived: she remembered the dinner and hurried into the kitchen to put the chops in the oven, and water to boil for the vegetables.

The worst ordeal was yet to come: the only way to retrieve the cups was to mingle with the men. Encouraged by the presence of Jock Craig at the bar, she lifted the flap and went through the gate, determined to brave the crowd. However, she needn't have worried: the soldiers stacked the crockery neatly and lifted the trays on to the counter, leaving her free to wipe the tables.

When she reached the far end of the room, one soldier was idly taking records out of their sleeves and then replacing them. 'Do you like music, miss? What can I play for you, Handel's *Largo*, the 1812, *Rose Marie*, or there's a nice selection from "New Moon"?'

Jessie plumped for the 1812, because it was the only piece she knew; the overture reverberated through the bar as she embarked on the washing up.

During dinner, Miss Taylor reprimanded her: the meal should have been ready at twelve forty-five and it was now one fifteen. Jessie apologised, explaining that it would have been on time if she hadn't made so many sandwiches.

'All twelve rounds!'

'No, it was a lot more than that. I did six before we opened, then another six. While you were making the tea, I did six more, and then there were six more after that.'

'You never did!'

'Do we need bread for the suppers tonight?'

'Of course we do!'

'Well, there's hardly any left; only enough for tea.'

Jessie showed the manageress the remains of the bread in the larder.

'Good heavens, is that all that's left? I'll have to borrow a loaf from the sergeant's mess.'

To ease the situation, Jessie related the snippets of conversation she had overheard when she was wiping the tables. 'The soldiers said the gravy was putrid and it was time the orderly corporal did something.'

Miss Taylor explained that the men were always complaining about the cookhouse food, but it must have been particularly bad that day or the men wouldn't have bought so many sandwiches. When Jessie pointed out that all the cakes had also been sold, she expressed surprise and fetched a box of biscuits from the grocery bar.

After dinner, Miss Taylor retired to the office, leaving Jessie to wash up and tidy the kitchen. As soon as she had finished, she quickly scribbled a note, to let her mother know her new address; then donned her working overall.

The mats in her bedroom were considerably improved by a good beating on the clothes-line in the yard and, after they had been scoured, the washbasin and chamber pot shone like new. She was in the process of scrubbing the floor when Miss Taylor appeared. 'What on earth are you doing? It's Sunday afternoon.'

'The floor was awful dirty and I thought it was better to scrub it before I put the polish on. I hope I didn't disturb you.'

'No, carry on, if it makes you happy.'

At four o'clock, Jessie was beginning to flag when Miss Taylor brought her a cup of tea and said that she could sit in the armchair in her room where there was a nice fire, but by the time she had had a wash and plaited her hair, it was getting late. She went to the kitchen to stoke up the range and was soon joined by the manageress, who prepared high tea, insisting that it was called supper.

One small matter had been worrying Jessie all afternoon. 'Do I have to pay for the Woodbines the soldier had this morning?'

'No, we have four shillings a day messing allowance, two shillings each. It can come out of that, unless, of course, you would like to clear the sink. Florrie didn't mind doing it.'

'I'd rather not, if you don't mind.'

'Well that's settled. It's a good job we don't open until six on Sundays.'

Miss Taylor went into the larder while Jessie washed up in the scullery. After a few minutes she came out again and went through the door into the yard saying, 'Whatever you do, make sure all foodstuff is covered with muslin.

41

One bluebottle in there and we could have a catastrophe. I shan't be long.'

Miss Taylor returned from the sergeant's mess carrying a loaf of bread, and in a very good humour. 'You'll find the laundry book on the dresser; the dirty linen's in the basket in your room.'

She obviously expected her instructions to be carried out straight away, so Jessie fetched the linen in order to itemise it. She offered to launder a pile of soiled underwear belonging to the previous assistant, but the manageress wouldn't hear of it. 'The best place for those is on the fire.' As soon as the bar opened, they were inundated with orders. Miss Taylor took a turn in the bar, leaving Jessie to cope in the kitchen. At a few minutes to eight, the manageress went to her bedroom and returned, wearing a pretty frock. 'The worst of the supper trade is over now. We never serve more than eight suppers, even on a busy night... If you want me, I'll be in the sergeant's mess. I've been invited across for a game of housey-housey.'

'What kind of game is that?'

'You pay tuppence for a card and each time one of your numbers is called, you mark it on the card. The first person to cross off all the numbers wins a prize.'

'What is the prize tonight?'

Miss Taylor laughed. 'That depends on the number of players. I suppose you could call it gambling, but the police can't do anything because we're on private property.'

'Before you go, would you crack some eggs for me?'

'You won't need them,' then seeing her assistant's consternation, 'all right, you can use them to make some rock cakes tomorrow.'

Left alone in the kitchen, Jessie made sure there was no one waiting at the counter; then sat down at the kitchen table. Her puritanical granny would not have approved if she had seen her cleaning her bedroom: she had always made a point of keeping the Sabbath Day holy. She was right of course: even the Naafi didn't include servile work in the Sunday duties. But scrubbing a floor was one thing, and gambling was another. Gambling was wrong on any day of the week... A knock on the counter caused her to abandon the moral debate.

An order for sausage and egg was followed, in quick succession, by three more for bacon and eggs. In her anxiety, Jessie forgot to swirl the first egg round in the cup before she tipped it out; it glided across the pan and spread in all directions. She tried to push it back into shape, to no avail: the white albumen stuck to the slice and the egg was soon covered in brown stringy strands. In a panic, she scraped the tangled mess on to a plate and wiped the pan with a piece of wrapping paper. The next three attempts were more successful, but now she had used all the eggs in the cups.

At nine o'clock, the bowl on the kitchen table contained five broken eggs, and Jessie dared not risk any more failures. Before the next customer had time to place an order she said, 'I'm sorry, there are no more eggs.'

'Perhaps it is just as well I don't like them,' said the soldier, in a cultured voice. 'Sausage sandwich cut in four please.'

She blushed and retreated to the kitchen.

The cooked sausages at first refused to part with their skins but, after a struggle, the sandwich looked fairly presentable. Jessie confidently placed it on the counter. The soldier lifted the bread to inspect the sausage. 'I see you have taken the skins off.'

'Did yi no want them aff?' In her anxiety Jessie lapsed into her native tongue.

'It was not my intention to criticise, but I can see that we will have to teach you to speak English.'

Lance Corporal Craig scowled across the bar. 'If all you can find fault with is Miss Edmondstone's accent, then there's nothing coming over you.'

'Just a joke, corporal, I meant no offence.'

By now the tables in the bar were littered with plates and cups. The kitchen was also in disarray: Jessie had used every available item of equipment to keep up with the demand. Fortunately, there was just enough time to do the washing up, and tidy the kitchen table, before the manageress returned at eleven.

'Did you manage all right?'

Jessie's eyes went to the bowl of eggs on the table.

'What in heaven's name is that?'

'Eggs,' Jessie replied, without looking up.

'But why didn't you use them up, like I showed you?'

'I was going to use them for the rock cakes tomorrow.'

'I don't know how many rock cakes you think you are going to make. There's enough there to make cakes for the entire barracks.'

'I'll pay for them.'

'You will not!'

There was no more to be said. Jessie asked if it was all right to go to bed. Miss Taylor retorted that she better had, or she wouldn't be fit for duty in the morning. It was past eleven o'clock.

Sergeant Brown called, 'Goodnight Jessie,' as she beat a hasty retreat.

5

The Yoke of the Yolks

The first Monday in February dawned cold, and dark enough to conceal the white layer of hoar frost that had settled on the Depot overnight. The bell on the alarm clock aroused Jessie from a deep sleep, but when she leapt out of bed, she was so intent on silencing the din that she wasn't immediately aware of the chill nip in the air. She pulled back the lined curtains and shivered as she noticed that the lighted doorway of the sergeant's mess was distorted by the frozen condensation on the windowpanes. There was less noise than usual: presumably, the mess door was shut to keep out the cold.

In the kitchen, Tibby stretched himself on the hearth, then rubbed his warm fur round her legs: he had obviously managed to sneak back in last night. Jessie gave him the last of yesterday's milk; then washed the jug and placed it on the shelf in the yard, ready for the next delivery.

It took the best part of an hour to clean the range because all the flues were clogged with soot, but the combination of the clean grate and sharp frost caused the wood to burn brightly. While the soldier was carrying out the massacre in the scullery, Jessie filled the kettle in the coffee bar, and also fetched a bowl of water to remove the layer of soot that had settled on the kitchen table.

At eight o'clock, Miss Taylor was still dozing and didn't

notice that her cup of tea was a quarter of an hour late. She stirred sufficiently to say, 'Thank you. Would you pass me those cigarettes?'

In the kitchen the fire was roaring up the chimney, so Jessie switched the heat over to the oven and placed the frying pan to warm. By the time the manageress had arrived, dressed in her white coat, the tinned tomatoes were hot and the bacon crisp. She commented that Jessie looked more like a chimney sweep than a general assistant, but she was pleased that the range had been polished with Enameline.

After breakfast, Miss Taylor gave a few hurried instructions because she had to open the grocery bar at nine o'clock. Jessie shook her sooty overall in the yard, and washed her face at the scullery sink; then went to the coffee bar. When she took down the shutters, she was surprised to find the tables and chairs stacked near the piano at the far end of the room, and a fire already laid in the black iron grate. A soldier, who was intent on mopping the floor, paused to say, 'Good morning'.

Jessie scrubbed the counter and set to work to clean the tarnished brass edge. The soldier passed her some glasses and advised her to open the door of the counter each morning: it was the custom to stack the crockery from the previous evening on the step.

The bar was reasonably clean and tidy, except for the floor behind the counter, which needed a scrub, but Jessie decided to ask first. Miss Taylor looked at her watch: it was too late to start on the kitchen floor, but there was just enough time to remove the layer of soot from the kitchen dresser and light the office fire.

At eleven o'clock the grocery bar closed and the manageress came into the kitchen to supervise. Jessie was sent to put on a clean overall; then she had to arrange the sandwiches and three dozen cakes on the stand in the bar. In the meantime, Miss Taylor had started to prepare the beverages, but made it clear that this was not her job.

A long blast on a horn, at twelve o'clock, was the signal for the men to go for their midday meal. Through the window, Jessie could see them crowding into the cookhouse, carrying their plates.

Ten minutes later, there was the sound of voices in the bar. The coffee was ready and the tea had brewed for exactly three minutes; there was just time to remove the tea bag and add the evaporated milk and sugar.

'Be quick now, the men have only a short break,' said the manageress, as Jessie carried the jug of tea into the bar.

The first customer wanted coffee. When Jessie fetched it from the kitchen, one of the soldiers was pouring six cups of tea. 'Don't look so worried, miss, I won't run away with the jug,' he said, as he put down sixpence.

A second soldier was helping to carry the cups to the table. 'We like our tea hot, miss. Tug's just making himself useful.'

When all the customers were sitting in groups around the tables, Jessie took the opportunity to peel some potatoes: she was out of sight when she stood beside the draining board in the alcove. She also managed to collect some of the crockery before she sat down to dinner, but there were now two piles of dirty dishes: one in the bar, the other in the scullery. Miss Taylor had cooked the dinner, but she hadn't done any washing up. She reminded Jessie that all the clearing up should be done before the general assistant went off duty. The bar menu was Sausage Toad, Fish Cakes and Rissoles; the cookery book was in the drawer, if she had forgotten what to do. There were two books in which to write the list of stock required, one for the coffee bar, the other for the kitchen. She would be in the grocery bar if anything were needed straight away.

Jessie decided to prepare the suppers first. This was relatively easy because the meat, left over from the Sunday joint, had to be minced, but the potatoes were already cooked. She knew how to make the batter for the Toad because her mother often allowed the family to make pancakes.

By three-thirty the bar, kitchen and scullery were all tidy. Jessie lay on her bed, covered with the feather eiderdown, admiring her handiwork of the previous afternoon. Miss Taylor had given her one of her own dressing-table mats to cover the stains on the chest of drawers, and two green vases from the cupboard in the kitchen, to use as ornaments. The floors had all to be washed in rotation and she wondered how long it would take. There was no point in lying in a cold room, with feet like blocks of ice, when the coffee bar was warm, and the floor was waiting to be scrubbed.

On Monday evening, Jessie took down the shutters feeling very pleased with herself. Miss Taylor had remarked that the whole range was hot, so the air must be circulating freely. She hadn't seen the bar floor yet, but it was obvious that she was pleased: she had lined up nine cups and, with a quick tap of a sharp knife, dropped one egg into each. Jessie had been dreading the fried suppers but now she was quite relieved. She was already fairly proficient at frying eggs, even if she hadn't mastered the art of breaking them.

Despite her optimism, a problem arose as soon as Jessie opened the bar: she knew the lance corporal's pint of bitter wasn't right as soon as she drew it. However, he said the firkin must be nearly empty and he would put up a new one to settle. A Whitbread would do, to be going on with; he would tap the new barrel tomorrow. He was apparently an authority on this subject, but he would have to come behind the bar, so she thought she had better obtain permission first.

The manageress and Sergeant Brown were sitting in the armchairs on either side of the glowing fire. Although Jessie apologised for the intrusion, she was given short shrift.

'I never get five minutes peace in this place. Drain off the last of the beer into the white enamel jug before Craig takes down the barrel.'

The humiliation made Jessie even more determined to use her initiative in future. However, her annoyance was short lived: the lance corporal was quick to notice the floor behind the counter, which 'had never been so clean'.

The cold weather resulted in an influx of soldiers, who came to warm themselves at the mess fire. Unfortunately, the smell of bacon and eggs was irresistible and soon a queue had formed. When the row of cups was empty, Jessie decided that the only way to perfect the art of egg-breaking was to practise.

Even with one casualty hidden under each success, there was still a surplus of broken eggs when Miss Taylor came into the kitchen at the end of the evening. She raised her hands and eyes in mock despair. 'Good heavens! Not more broken eggs.'

Having made her final round of inspection, she enquired, 'Where did you put the jug of beer?'

'I threw it away.'

Once again she was exasperated. How could she account for the beer she hadn't seen?

'But it made the bar smell.'

'Never do that again! Stale beer must be measured before it's written off. It'll be your fault if I have a bad stock.' She flounced into her bedroom, leaving Jessie to switch off the lights.

Tuesday evening was another fiasco: the dozen eggs, left in readiness, failed to meet the demand. On her return, Miss Taylor's face was flushed, her speech slightly slurred. 'And what am I shupposed to do with theshe?' She pointed to the bowl on the table.

Sergeant Brown was sympathetic. 'Perhaps it's the shells. If the hens don't have lime in their feed, the shells are fragile.'

'Nonsense! She's just not trying.'

The sergeant decided it was time to say, 'Goodnight'.

Miss Taylor darted after him. 'You're not going, Cyril, without a drink?'

As he hesitated, Jessie willed him to stay, but he decided it was late and took his leave.

The following day, the manageress busied herself in the grocery bar throughout the morning, only coming into the kitchen once, to give instructions about the bar menu. She was in no mood for conversation at dinner time, so Jessie washed up and went to bed.

She awoke to find Miss Taylor standing at the bedroom door.

'I'm sorry, were you asleep? I missed my half-day last week. I'll be going out as soon as I close. You'll only have yourself to cater for at supper time.'

On the stroke of five the manageress closed the grocery, went to her bedroom and returned, almost immediately, dressed in her outdoor clothes. At the door of the scullery, she hesitated, then came back into the kitchen and took six cups from the dresser. As she cracked an egg in each,

50

she said, 'These should be enough to last you all evening. We're never very busy on a Wednesday.'

Jessie was dismayed: her superior had forestalled her. On her first evening, Miss Taylor had mentioned that Florrie had refused to cook eggs. If the previous assistant had the right to object, so had she.

Lance Corporal Craig was first in the bar, listening intently to another soldier, who had just returned from a course. The young man walked across to study the menu, then looked at the display of sandwiches on the stand. The lance corporal decided to assist. 'Miss Edmondstone does a nice line in bacon and eggs.'

Normally, Jessie would have been pleased with the compliment, but at this particular moment, the remark placed her on the horns of a dilemma: if the soldier chose bacon and eggs, she would have to oblige for the sake of her mentor's prestige. On the other hand, one fried supper would set a precedent and she would be hard put to refuse any other requests.

'Bacon, eggs, bread and butter with a cup of tea,' said the soldier, to her dismay.

After he had been served, there were only four eggs left, therefore the problem, posed by the fragile shells, would have to be tackled before the next customers arrived. Jessie placed an egg in the palm of her hand and tapped it so gently with a knife that the shell fractured but the white membrane remained intact. As she tried to prise the two halves apart, the membrane suddenly yielded under the pressure of her thumbs: the yolk disintegrated. She tried again, without success. In despair, she clasped her hands together and said aloud, 'Please, please, help me.' At that moment, she had a vivid flash of memory: her mother cracked an egg on the rim of a saucer and pulled the shell apart with her fingertips. Jessie fetched a saucer and emulated the single swift action: the yolk remained intact.

51

Flushed with success, Jessie stopped to admire the battalion of ten eggs, lined up two abreast on the far side of the table. Suddenly, she was seized with panic as a thought occurred to her: supposing no one wanted eggs that evening!

It seemed like an eternity before Private Pompey inadvertently came to the rescue with an order for bacon, eggs and tomatoes. After that, the requests came in quick succession. For once, she was grateful that there was no respite.

At eleven o'clock the manageress returned. 'Well, how many omelettes do we have to eat tomorrow?' There was a note of sarcasm in her voice.

Jessie shrugged. 'None.'

'Well, where are the broken ones?'

'I managed to crack them without breaking them tonight.'

'There you are. What did I tell you?' She turned to Sergeant Brown. 'These girls are all alike: if they can find someone else to do the work for them, they won't bother to try.'

The sergeant made no comment, but as he said, 'Goodnight', the almost imperceptible flutter of his left eyelid conveyed the impression that he didn't entirely agree.

6

No Christian Names

As a rule, the wages of the Naafi staff were paid on Friday, but on Jessie's first half-day, Miss Taylor decided to pay her a day in advance. At three-thirty, she boarded the train for Southport, eventually arriving at the main shopping centre, Lord Street. She wandered aimlessly along the boulevard, and soon lost interest in the expensive goods on display: she had slipped a ten-shilling note into the envelope before she posted a letter to her mother.

At the cinema, she joined the long queue waiting for the next house, but changed her mind when the biting wind caused her face and hands to sting.

In the window of a tea shop there was a selection of iced fancies and Eccles cakes. The tables at the back of the shop looked very inviting with their brightly coloured cloths, but there were no prices, and she wasn't sure if she could pay for one cup, or if she would be expected to order a tray of tea. By now, there were flakes of snow in the wind and she longed for the warmth of the kitchen range. The thought of a fire jogged her memory: there was a cheery blaze in the waiting room at the station. She wasn't due back at the canteen until eleven, so there was no need to catch a train until ten o'clock. Four hours was too long to sit in the waiting room, but there was nothing else to do.

Back at the station, Jessie purchased a bar of chocolate

from a man with a trolley and settled herself by the fire. A middle-aged lady soon joined her, remarking that she wouldn't be surprised if there was a heavy fall of snow. At first, Jessie was pleased to have company, but when the stranger started to question her about her home and her work, she decided that the lady was too inquisitive, and went to find out the departure times of the trains.

It was dark when Jessie arrived at Burscough, but two soldiers were ahead of her as she left the station, so she tailed them back to the barracks, keeping her distance.

In the kitchen, Miss Taylor was frying bacon. 'Goodness, you are back early,' she exclaimed. 'Did you buy anything?'

'There was nothing I particularly needed.'

'I thought you'd gone to the pictures.'

'I'd already seen it.'

'That's what you call a canny Scot!' The remark was addressed to Sergeant Brown, who was sitting at the table, reading a newspaper.

'What are you going to do now?' The manageress thought for a moment. 'You can't sit in your bedroom without a fire. I'll tell you what you can do: go and sit in my armchair and read the magazines.'

It was a real treat to relax in the armchair and read the *People's Friend*. When Jessie finished the third love story, she sat back to watch the flickering flames. It was ten o'clock and she could still hear the clatter of dishes, so she decided to show her appreciation by returning the favour.

The kitchen table had been cleared, but the pile of tins on the draining board in the scullery was visible through the open door. Jessie changed into her overall and set to work. Miss Taylor came to see what was happening and expressed her gratitude. 'I've never known it to be so busy on a Thursday: the cold weather has doubled the trade.'

'Has Sergeant Brown gone?'

'Yes, I hadn't a minute to spare. He's having an early night.'

Jessie sympathised, but she was pleased that her own lateness, on the two previous evenings, was not entirely due to incompetence.

On Friday morning, Jessie had just switched on the kitchen light when there was a tap on the kitchen window. Her curiosity aroused, she lifted the bar and pushed open the window to find the army cook, shivering in the yard.

'Miss, I'm absolutely gasping for a cigarette. Could you let me have a Players please?'

Jessie hesitated.

'Please, miss.'

The grocery bar would not be open until nine o'clock and it was now only seven. She took his sixpence and fetched the cigarettes.

Throughout the morning, Jessie kept thinking about the coin beside the cigarettes in the drawer. She wouldn't know what to say if asked to account for it. At lunchtime, she remembered to put the money in the float, but there was still the possibility that the cook would mention the purchase when he collected the army rations.

At two o'clock Jessie lingered near the door of the grocery. The manageress rhymed off the list of ingredients. 'Sign here please.' The cook carried the stores out to his barrow and set off round the building.

With a sigh of relief, Jessie settled down by the kitchen range to read the rest of the articles in the magazines. She had already decided to open the bar punctually, to be ready for the onslaught.

Apart from the lance corporal, there were only two customers in the coffee bar during the first half hour, but the evening was considerably enlivened by the arrival of Private Riley, wearing a good quality grey suit and trilby hat. The royal blue nap coat, neatly folded over his arm; the sharp creases in his trousers; a well-laundered pale blue shirt and shining shoes all contributed to his immaculate appearance.

'What's your name?' he enquired, with a charming smile.

'Miss Edmondstone,' was the curt reply. Jessie had so many misgivings about breaking one rule that she was determined not to break another.

'No, your Christian name.'

'I'm Miss Edmondstone.'

'Sure and you're the only girl I know without a first name. Are you a Christian?'

She nodded.

'Then you must have a Christian name. Would it be Margaret ... or Mary ... or Ann?' He studied her quizzically as he mentioned a few more.

If she said 'no' to each guess, he would eventually find out by a process of elimination, so she decided not to answer.

Jock Craig rescued her by calling for a pint, but as soon as she was free again, Private Riley came to the counter to buy a bar of chocolate, as an excuse to continue the one-sided conversation.

'The Irish and the Scots are the Celtic races, so I can easily manage to say Miss Edmondstone, but most of the men will be finding it difficult to grapple with a name like that.' He shook his head dolefully, then his face lit up as if he had just received a flash of inspiration. 'With sparkling eyes like that, it can only be Bright Eyes.'

Jessie was completely disarmed by his tactics. 'Oh no,' she said, as she glanced towards the kitchen.

'You're surely not frightened of Molly, with her Irish temper.'

'No, but...'

'You don't want to take any notice of her, her bark is worse than her bite.'

Anxious that Miss Taylor might hear, Jessie made an excuse about the food needing attention and sought refuge in the kitchen.

Private Riley tried several more times to become better acquainted, but each attempt was thwarted by the arrival of a customer. Finally, he gave up and called, 'Goodbye Mavoureen,' as he left the bar.

Throughout the evening Jessie was never idle, but the pace was more leisurely. When she went to bed, she lay awake thinking about Private Riley. Although she was flattered by his attention, she knew that if he found out her name, he wouldn't hesitate to use it and Miss Taylor would be cross.

On Saturday morning, Jessie was washing up the breakfast dishes when a soldier called at the back door. He was dressed in army uniform, but the special band on his arm showed he was the postman. Mam had replied by return of post because she was so pleased with the ten-shilling note. She was still doing the washing and was hoping to save the fare to visit John in London. Her stomach was much better now. Jessie mused that this affliction usually disappeared when her financial state improved. The letter made Jessie feel slightly homesick: she had been at Burscough only one week, but it seemed much longer.

After dinner, Jessie was finishing the clearing up when Miss Taylor came into the kitchen, wearing a smart navy-blue suit, matching shoes and gloves, and carrying an expensive leather handbag. Although the suit was tailored, the severity of the style was relieved by a small fur necklet, slung casually round her shoulders, and a toque with a flatteringly ruched veil. When Jessie complimented her on her appearance, she was obviously pleased, but her manner was brisk as she gave her last-minute instructions.

'Now, you know what to do. Saturday is always slack, so you'll be all right. I've left the grocery bar door unlocked, just in case you're short of anything, but on no account must you forget to write it down. If you need any change, it's in the desk in the office. Now, is there anything you want before I go?'

'Will you be back for high tea?'

'Supper, you mean, no, Cyril and I will be having afternoon tea in town before we go to a show. Is there anything else?'

'I don't think so.'

'You'll remember to make up my fire.'

'I'll try not to forget.'

'You'd better not. I must remember to put in a complaint about that coal. How anyone can be expected to heat a range with that rubbish, I do not know.'

Jessie tried to think of anything she might need as Miss Taylor pulled on her kid gloves.

'Don't look so worried. You seem to get on all right with Corporal Craig. He's the only one likely to cause trouble.'

After a polite exchange of good wishes for a nice afternoon, Jessie was once again alone, but there was no time for self-pity: she would take the opportunity to have a good wash in her bedroom. The staff were allowed to shower in the sergeant's mess, but Miss Taylor had already voiced her objections: apart from the fact that she would have to make arrangements in advance, she would not suffer the embarrassment of walking across the public path, carrying her towel. Jessie was also unwilling to make use of the facilities: she was too shy to submit a request, let alone brave the unknown territory across the yard.

However, there was no point in having a wash until the fires had been stoked and the coalscuttles filled ready for the morning. In the shed, Jessie wielded the heavy hammer in an attempt to break up the solid lumps. The chips flew in all directions, but the largest lump resisted her efforts to break it. She was just about to give up when it fractured; then it was comparatively easy to pound it down to reasonably sized pieces. She carried the scuttles into the kitchen, spread the sticks out on the hearth to dry, and checked that the coal on the office fire had caught alight.

The kitchen would be left unattended, but the only visitors to come through the back door were the farmer, who delivered the milk, the soldier on fatigues, and the butcher. They had all come early in the morning. The only other person to use the door was Sergeant Brown and his movements had already been accounted for. Having taken the precaution of bolting the yard door, nothing else required immediate attention.

After a good wash down, Jessie brought her underwear to the scullery; then remembered there was no soap powder. There was a small packet of Hudson's in the grocery, but it was the custom to show any proposed purchases to the charge hand or manageress. She decided to use a handful of the canteen soda and her own tablet of Lifebuoy soap.

Two cotton chemises, two petticoats and two liberty bodices were soon dripping on the line in the yard, but Jessie wrung out her blue fleecy lined knickers as tightly as she could, and draped them over the cylinder in the scullery. There wasn't enough time left to prepare her own meal, so she put the pennies in the cash box and ate two bars of hazelnut chocolate as she prepared the sandwiches.

Promptly, at five-thirty, she took down the first shutter and was confronted by a soldier, with his freshly washed hair standing on end. 'Sorry to trouble you, miss, but could I have a jar of Pomade?'

'In the drawer with the Vaseline,' said Jock Craig.

'Thanks, miss,' said the soldier. As he paid her, he added, 'you'll have to come to the dance on your night off.'

Jock Craig offered to buy Jessie a Guinness. When she refused, he commented that she was not like her predecessor – not that he had ever offered to buy her a drink.

Miss Taylor's prediction that she wouldn't be busy wasn't fulfilled: bacon and eggs had become very popular and Jessie was thankful that she could now break the eggs herself. She had no qualms about being alone in the kitchen, until she heard a noise in the office and went to investigate. The fire was out and the cat was curled up on Miss Taylor's bed.

As she carried Tibby through the dark scullery there was a crunching sound underfoot. She fetched the broom from the yard to sweep out the cockroaches, but by the time she returned, the light had sent them scurrying under the skirting board.

In the bar some new arrivals were trying to attract her attention, but later in the evening there was a lull and she managed to stay in the office until the wood had kindled and the coal was beginning to glow.

Back in the bar, Private Riley was standing beside the counter, dressed in khaki. 'Hello Josephine,' he said.

'Are you speaking to me?' Jessie enquired as she gazed around at the empty space behind the counter.

'Sorry, I forgot your name is Janet.' He was hoping that she would automatically correct him, but she ignored the mistake.

'Did you want something?'

'Yes, a bar of chocolate please, ... Joan.' He scrutinised her face as he added the name to his request, but Jessie's expression didn't change. He paid for the chocolate and waited until she started to walk away.

'Joyce,' he called. The name was so similar to Jess that her head turned in an involuntary movement, then, regaining her self-control, she pivoted slowly on her heel. 'Did you want me?' The emphasis was firmly on 'me'.

'Yes Juliana, I forgot to ask for a cup of tea.'

'Will you stop calling me all those names, I'm Miss Edmondstone,' she said, in an effort to put him in his place.

He glanced across at Jock Craig. 'Sure now, I wouldn't dare to call you names in front of all your admirers.'

'Well, stop bothering me then,'

'Sure I will, if you'll just tell me your first name.'

'I'm not allowed to.'

'Well, Florrie was called Florrie, so I can't see why you can't be called...' He paused, waiting for Jessie to fill in the missing word.

'You can go on trying your tricks, but you won't get it out of me.'

'Sure and I'm already half-way there: your name begins with J.'

'How did you find that out?' Jessie was so surprised that the question came spontaneously.

'I have friends in high places,' he said, as he smiled across at the postman, who was sitting at one of the tables. Having scored a point, the private sat down to consider his next move. One of his compatriots said he might as well give up. It was just a waste of time.

'Sure now, haven't I all the time in the world?' he said airily, and remained at the table for the rest of the evening. Each time Jessie went out to collect the cups, he gave her a saucy wink.

It was almost closing time when the philandering Irishman came to the counter again. All trace of frivolity had disappeared as he said earnestly, 'You really are unkind, you know.'

'Why?' she enquired, as if she didn't already know.

'You still haven't told me your name, and after me giving up a whole evening for you.'

'Oh, you didn't. I bet you're on duty.' It was a long shot but it caused him to chuckle.

'Whoever told you that?'

'I think you're terrible, Private Riley.' She couldn't help being amused by his audacity.

'I like the ways you roll your rr's. Just say it again and, cross my heart, I won't ever ask your name again.'

'Say what again?'

'I think you're terrible, Paddy Riley.'

Everyone in the bar called him Paddy and Jessie was so familiar with his name that she repeated the sentence without noticing that he had changed one word.

'There you are Mavoureen, now we are on such friendly terms, should you not be allowing me the privilege of using your other name.'

'But you've just promised not to ask my name.'

'But if you are going to call me Paddy, I can hardly call you Miss Edmondstone.'

'But you promised.'

'That was before you showed your true feelings for me.'

Jessie turned away and started to put up the shutters in order to hide her blushes.

Jock Craig said his usual, 'Goodnight, Miss Edmondstone.'

'Goodnight, corporal,' she replied.

'And goodnight, Paddy,' said her tormentor, with a mischievous grin as he walked backwards through the door.

It was ten-thirty when Jessie sat down to drink a cup of cocoa. Miss Taylor wouldn't mind if she went to bed, but perhaps she had better wait up until she returned. She crossed her arms on the table to rest her head.

* * *

In the distance there was a thumping and banging, followed by a sharp rap on the window. As Miss Taylor's puce face gradually came into focus, Jessie was bewildered by her gesticulations, but when she opened the casement, there was no mistaking the peremptory command. 'Go and unbolt the door of the backyard at once.'

She rushed outside and struggled to undo the rusty bolt. The manageress pushed the door open and marched in, followed by Sergeant Brown. 'What do you mean by bolting the yard door? I'm sure we must have roused the whole Depot trying to attract your attention. And pray, what are you doing, sitting here with all the lights on?' She looked around suspiciously. 'Have you had someone in here?'

'Oh no, no one.'

It was not until that moment that Jessie recalled the events of the afternoon and her cheeks flushed as a thought crossed her mind: Sergeant Brown must have seen her faded blue knickers as he came through the scullery. Seeing her consternation, the manageress persisted, 'Are you sure?'

'Yes, I'm quite sure.' She was so positive that the manageress didn't question her further.

'You'd better go!'

Jessie went to the scullery, grabbed her knickers and looked frantically around, but there was nowhere to hide them. At the scullery door, she waited for an opportunity to cross the kitchen, but Miss Taylor was offering the sergeant a cup of cocoa and they were likely to be there for some time. She undid the top button of her overall and stuffed the knickers inside. As she walked swiftly across the kitchen, Sergeant Brown had his back towards her, but Miss Taylor gazed in astonishment at her expanded bosom.

'Goodnight, Jessie,' called the sergeant.

'Goodnight,' she replied, without turning her head.

As she walked along the passage, Jessie couldn't help overhearing Miss Taylor's remark. 'She's a most peculiar girl.'

'Perhaps she's frightened of the dark. It must be lonely once the bar is closed.'

Sergeant Brown always sprang to her defence. He really was a gentleman.

7

The Baptism

Three weeks had elapsed since Jessie's arrival at Burscough, when a slightly disgruntled Miss Taylor announced that the accountant would be coming on the following Monday, which meant she would lose her Saturday half-day yet again. As soon as she received the notification, she pinned a notice on the door to advise the customers that the grocery bar would be closed on Monday morning; then spent every spare minute taking stock.

The commodities in the coffee bar were kept to a minimum, to facilitate checking, but when the bar closed on Sunday evening, at the usual time, there was still a great deal to be done. Full cartons of cigarettes were stacked according to brand, and loose packets were placed on top of the corresponding pile. The display on the stand was dismantled; even the white cotton covers were laid aside. It was not until the contents of every cupboard and drawer had been checked and labelled with scraps of paper that they both retired, very late, to bed.

On Monday morning, Jessie awoke early because Miss Taylor's nervousness had subconsciously affected her. The manageress had been irritable for the past few days, and had even lost her temper with Sergeant Brown when he was trying to help her by lifting the sugar and potato sacks on to the scales.

At breakfast they were both tired. As the manageress chain-smoked her third cigarette, Jessie tactlessly remarked that her fingers were becoming very stained with nicotine. She retorted that she had had enough of Cyril lecturing her, so Jessie retreated to the scullery with the breakfast dishes.

Promptly, at nine o'clock, there was a tap on the glass panel of the grocery door. Miss Taylor went through to admit a slightly stooped figure.

In the office, the elderly gentleman divested himself of his overcoat, bowler hat and umbrella to reveal a neat grey suit, matching shirt and what seemed to be a regimental tie with an attractive pattern, despite the subdued colours. With the brief announcement that he would begin in the coffee bar, he immediately set to work. Jessie wasn't sure if her presence was required so she lingered as he checked that the scraps of paper tallied with the actual quantities. When he began to write in his ledger, she decided not to waste any more time and set off with the intention of making her bed. As she passed the door of the grocery, Miss Taylor suggested that they would all enjoy a cup of tea. 'When you take a tray to Mr Ford, ask him if he will take lunch. He never does, but ask him all the same.'

Jessie gave the manageress a cup of tea then carried the tray into the coffee bar. 'Mr Ford,' she said nervously. The accountant made it abundantly clear that he didn't welcome interruptions: he raised his hand as if to halt any further utterance and continued his work. Jessie waited: if he wanted lunch, it would have to be prepared soon. After a seemingly long time, he pointed to a pile of boxes. 'Remove those top three cartons.'

Jessie picked up the Players, Capstan and Weights, and waited patiently for further instructions, which were not forthcoming because the accountant was again immersed in his work. It was only when she began to push some other stock aside, to make room for the cartons that he glanced at her. 'Don't touch them. Put those on the floor.'

66

Jessie watched as he opened the remaining cartons of Woodbine, Brown Cat, Senior Service and a new brand called Ardath.

'You can close those boxes,' he said, without looking up as he recorded the totals in his book; then walked towards the beer bar. As Jessie hadn't yet invited him to lunch, she followed, in the hope that there would be a convenient pause in the proceedings.

'Where's the dip stick, miss?'

The accountant's eyebrows rose as he inspected the gleaming brass stick. Jessie took the opportunity to enquire, 'Do you want lunch, sir?'

For a moment, Jessie thought he was going to say 'yes', but then he seemed to change his mind. 'No thank you, just a cup of tea.'

The checking of the kitchen stock did not take long, but Jessie was still in the midst of her preparations when the horn sounded. Minutes later, the first customers arrived in the bar.

'Hello, what's happened to the display stand?'

'I'll bet its stock-taking, am I right, miss?'

Jessie nodded as she searched for a stick of shaving soap amongst the miscellany of items still on the stand.

As soon as the main rush was over, Jessie went into the kitchen to lay the table.

She was summoned, almost immediately, by a rat-a-tat: in the bar Paddy Riley and Blondie, the assistant cook, were standing at the counter. Blondie wanted cigarettes; Paddy requested tea and cakes.

'Not another stock-taking? It's not long since you had one,' remarked Blondie.

Jessie corrected him. 'No, this is my first one.'

'That's right, it was Florrie who was complaining she got no overtime.'

'You should mention it to the supervisor, miss.'

67

'Sure, she can't complain. Doesn't she hop out of bed just in time to make the tae and then she goes straight back again as soon as she's done the washing up.'

'I'll have you know, Private Riley, I got up at seven o'clock this morning.'

'Sure, I know you did not.'

'I'm not going to argue with you, Private Riley, just give me your money. I'm very busy.'

'Say please, Paddy.'

'Please, Private Riley.'

He handed over sixpence. 'Your eyes sparkle when you're annoyed.'

'Och, go away with you.'

As Jessie served the queue, she ignored Paddy and Blondie, but their banter was intended for her ears.

'Sure now, wasn't she improperly dressed?'

'No cap.'

'And no tie. It's a good job the orderly corporal didn't see her or he'd have put her on a charge.'

'Oh, but he did see her.'

'What happened?'

'He couldn't fill out the charge sheet.'

'Why was that then?'

'She refused to give her Christian name.'

'Did he report her to the C.O.?'

'Yes.'

'What did she get?'

'He was going to give her three months C.B.'

'Then why didn't he?'

'He couldn't spell Edmondstone, so he let her off with a caution.'

When all the customers had been served, Jessie turned towards the kitchen.

'A bar of Duncan's, please, miss.' Paddy prevented her withdrawal.

As she took his sixpence he said, 'We are still friends, aren't we now, Mavoureen?'

'Yes, but I did get up at seven o'clock this morning.'

'Sure you did not. It wasn't seven o'clock when we saw her, was it Blondie?'

'No, I have to agree with you Paddy,' said Blondie, apologetically.

'Weren't we in the cookhouse when she came into the kitchen?'

'Yes.'

'There she was, yawning her head off – she would have fallen asleep if she hadn't been leaning on the broom.'

'Well, if I was sweeping the floor, I had already cleaned the range, so it must have been seven o'clock,' she said triumphantly.

'No, you're making a mistake.' Paddy shook his head. 'It wasn't a minute after quarter to seven, was it Blondie?'

'Och, yi really are terrible, Private Riley!'

Paddy responded with his usual saucy wink.

Mr Ford was still working in the grocery bar, but not long afterwards he retired to the office with a third cup of tea.

Jessie was busy putting the coffee bar back to rights, unaware of the accountant's departure until Miss Taylor came to tell her that he had just gone. 'Thank God, the stock's all right.'

Jessie thought this was a foregone conclusion. 'How long will it be before the next one?'

'That depends – I suppose about six weeks as the books are in order.'

The next morning Miss Taylor was late for breakfast; although she was in better spirits, she looked pale and drawn. Business was brisk in the grocery bar, but when there was a few minutes respite, she came into the kitchen and asked Jessie to keep an eye on things while she went into the yard.

The shop bell rang almost immediately. Jessie went to greet the customer, but didn't recognise the corpulent civilian who was closing the door behind him. Instead of waiting at the counter, he lifted the flap and unbolted the door. Jessie's heart missed a beat as he glanced at the notes and silver in the cash box, which was usually kept closed. In a panic, she looked across at the cookhouse: if he took the box, she would have to raise the alarm quickly. By now, the stranger was systematically securing the door of the counter. Although he wore a gabardine mackintosh, he had the upright bearing of a soldier.

'What is your name?' he enquired, as he strode into the kitchen.

'Miss Edmondstone.'

'I'm Mr Johnson, the Area Manager. Is Miss Taylor in her office?'

'No sir, she's in the yard.'

He walked towards the scullery, but evidently thought better of it, and waited near the door. Miss Taylor came in the back door and washed her hands, unaware of his arrival. As she came into the kitchen she said, 'I thought I told you to mind the shop.' Then, noticing the visitor, 'Oh, good morning, Mr Johnson.' The shop bell rang. 'If you'll excuse me, I'd better attend to the shop first.'

'I've got rather a lot to do this morning,' he said impatiently, and turned to Jessie. 'Have you ever served in a shop?'

'Yes, sir.'

'Well take over the grocery bar for a few minutes.'

A soldier was the only customer in the grocery. He was soon served because he only wanted cigarettes, but he held the door open for a woman carrying two large

70

shopping bags. She fumbled in her pocket and produced a long shopping list.

The tea and sugar were already weighed. Jessie placed a $^1/_2$ lb brown bag and 2 lb blue bag on the counter.

'Half a pound of butter and half a pound of margarine.'

The wooden slats were in a white bowl, decorated with a cow grazing under a tree. The water dripped off the grooved wood as Jessie steadied the butter with the slat in her left hand and took a swipe with her right. The hard surface of the butter was only slightly dented, so she gripped one slat with two hands and used it as a chopper to hack her way through; then pressed hard. The butter divided suddenly, causing the smaller piece to skid across the wet marble and rebound on the glazed surround. As she started to pat it into shape, the woman remarked that she only wanted half a pound. Instead of heeding the implied criticism, she continued to pat the butter and placed it on the scale. The woman sniffed as the brass pan descended with a thud. 'I said I only want half a pound. That's at least a pound.'

To Jessie's relief, Miss Taylor returned. 'I'll see to it, if you fill the small kettle.'

As she placed the kettle on the hob, she could hear the laughter in the grocery bar; the voices were still raised when the hilarity subsided.

'How are you dear?'

'Not too good.'

'You really ought to go to the doctor.'

'I wouldn't know what to say. It's a pity there aren't any women doctors.'

Miss Taylor served one more customer, then it was time to close the bar. She came through to lay a tray for Mr Johnson, who remained in the office while Jessie prepared for the twelve o'clock opening.

In the bar, Jock Craig was leaning on the counter as

usual, but he straightened himself up as Mr Johnson entered. Miss Taylor grimaced at Jessie when she saw her arch-enemy in conversation with the Area Manager, who kept looking in Jessie's direction and rubbing his chin, as if considering what to do. He joined Miss Taylor in the office, but it was not long before they both returned. He beckoned to Jessie. 'Miss Edmondstone, this is a small canteen and it doesn't pay for itself. I realise that there is quite a lot of work for two people, but the canteen will not support another member of staff. I have decided to send you a trainee. That should help.'

In the bar that evening, Jessie was telling Jock Craig how delighted she was at the prospect of having an assistant, when Paddy Riley arrived and sat down at one of the tables. She was just about to go through the counter to collect the cups when he came to request 'a cup of tae'. He stood, waiting for his tea to cool, then said, 'Could I have a teaspoon please, miss?'

Jessie gave it to him, keeping her distance.

'Would you come a bit closer? I'd like to have a word with you.'

There was a note of urgency in his voice, so she stepped towards him and leaned on the counter to listen. He dipped his finger in the tea cup and adroitly made the sign of the cross on her forehead, saying with all due solemnity, 'I baptise thee Scottie.'

Taken by surprise, she drew back, unable to conceal her amusement as she wiped the tea from her forehead. 'I'm no' a wee dog on a whisky bottle,' she said as she turned away.

Jock Craig made it clear that he didn't approve. 'Less of the blarney, Riley,' he said gruffly.

Paddy was unabashed and replied with his usual good humour, 'I can't have my second-best girl without a name, corporal.'

Jock Craig didn't reply, but he was definitely out of temper. Jessie had grown quite fond of the big Scotsman and was dismayed by his morose expression. She was also surprised at the vehemence of his reaction to such a harmless joke.

8

The Trainee Assistant

The March winds came in gusts, causing a downdraught, which put a damper on the fire, therefore extra wood was needed to encourage the flame and speed up the kettle. Jessie opened the back door and found the concrete enclosure strewn with old invoices, snatched from the chest and scattered in all directions by the wind. In the dark coalhouse, the pungent spray of the cat caused her to hold her breath while she extricated the wood from the sack.

Back in the kitchen, the air was warm, but Jessie shivered as she bent over the range and carefully criss-crossed the sticks to lure the flame towards the hob. Her patience was rewarded: it was not long before the wood was sparking and crackling.

At breakfast Jessie waited patiently as the manageress sorted through the pile of circulars to unearth two letters. Every week, a letter arrived with the address written in a large scrawl, but neither the contents nor the sender were ever revealed. However, Jessie recognised the writing on the second envelope and remained at the table because she knew she would be told the news.

Miss Taylor finished reading the second letter. 'Mrs Hadley sends you her regards. She says Gwyneth is getting married next month.'

Jessie sighed. 'She's very lucky, she's so pretty and rich.'

'Rich? Who told you that?'

'Gwyneth did.'

'Nonsense! Her father's a miner. They live in a cottage, one up and one down.'

'But she has lovely clothes.'

'So would you, if you spent all your money on yourself. Now, while I think of it, I'll have to go to the post office after lunch, and I don't know what time the new assistant will arrive. I doubt if she'll be here before two, but if she comes, you can make her a cup of tea.'

Each week, Miss Taylor made about three visits to the village, usually between twelve and two when the grocery bar was closed, presumably to send off the takings, but she was always careful not to disclose her business.

After Jessie closed the coffee bar, she went to the office to light the fire. As she carried the pan of ash along the passage, a woman's voice called, 'Anyone at home?'

In the kitchen, a plump woman was standing beside the table. 'Are you the charge hand?' she enquired.

'No, the general assistant.'

'Do you mind if I sit down? It's quite a long walk from the station.' Without waiting for an answer, she deposited her bag on the kitchen table and made herself comfortable on the nearest chair. 'What's your name?'

'Miss Edmondstone. Miss Taylor doesn't like familiarity with the troops.'

'Oh, she's one of those, is she?'

Jessie hastened to add, 'She's really nice. She calls me Jessie.'

'I could drink a cup of tea,' said the visitor.

Jessie filled the kettle and poked the fire.

'It would be quicker on the gas.'

'We have no gas.'

'No gas! Who lights the fire and cleans the kitchen range?

76

'I do.'

'Are the chimneys swept often?'

'The sweep told me he comes every four to six months.'

'Are you leaving then?'

'No.'

'Well, what exactly do you do in the way of duties?'

Jessie presumed she must be the expected trainee and explained the routine. As she made the tea, she couldn't help surmising that the woman was her senior by several years. Her peroxide blonde hair was dark at the roots; her features were quite attractive, despite her plump cheeks and double chin, but her posture marred any pretensions to elegance. The care that she had expended on her make-up was completely wasted: she slouched on the chair, with knees apart, and one foot leaning outward at the ankle.

Jessie poured the tea. The trainee stretched across the table to take the china cup, leaving the delft. Then she lit a cigarette and rested it on the saucer while she patted her coiffed hair. 'The wind has ruined my hair. I'll have to tidy up after I've had this cup of tea.'

Miss Taylor's arrival put an end to any further conversation. 'Jessie, would you open the grocery door? Corporal Smythe is waiting outside.'

By the time Jessie had unbolted the door, the manageress was pulling on her white coat. 'The rations are at the end of the counter.'

The army cook carried the provisions out to the barrow and returned to sign the chit. Jessie diplomatically left Miss Taylor to rejoin the trainee and set to work in the coffee bar.

'The manageress said you'd find me an overall.' The new assistant startled a pensive Jessie. 'So this is the coffee bar! I see you sell Guinness.'

'Yes, it's the coffee and beer bar combined. We sell beer, but no spirits.'

On the way to the bedroom, Jessie collected a uniform from the linen cupboard in the passage. When the overall was unfolded, it was obvious that it wouldn't fit, so she went to find a larger size and returned with the whole pile. The trainee was trying on the first overall, but the blue cotton drill was reluctant to envelop her large bosom. She struggled out of it and into another. The buttons on the bodice fastened with a grudge; the belt stretched round her girth, but there was no overlap to allow the button to reach the buttonhole. As she twisted round in front of the mirror to view the back of the skirt, riding up over her hips, she said, 'I've put on so much weight since I gave up smoking. That's why I've decided to take it up again.' She selected another overall. This time, the garment fitted perfectly and the blue fabric flattered her eyes. Jessie was just about to pay her a compliment when she ruined the whole effect by slapping the cap on the back of her head and securing it with two hairpins. Next, she rummaged inside her travelling case and produced a pair of curling tongs; then she hesitated, 'Oh dear, there's no gas.'

'You can heat them at the kitchen range.'

'I don't want my hair to be black with soot.'

'You can put them in the red part of the fire. There's some wrapping paper in the dresser if you want to test them.'

'I won't bother now, thank you all the same. What did you say your name was?'

'Jessie,' she said, as she removed the bedspread to reveal the freshly laundered blankets.

'My name is Veronica, but you can call me Vera, for short.'

'I can't call you by your Christian name in the bar. What is your other name?'

'Mrs Shane.' She started to buffer her oval fingernails.

'I'd better call you Mrs Shane at first, so I don't forget. Is there anything else you want?'

'No, that will be all.'

By the time her new assistant came to the kitchen, Jessie had prepared the liver casserole and placed the meat puddings in the steamer.

'I'll use my curling tongs, if you don't mind.' Vera poked the fire; then stood, looking around the kitchen. 'There's no mirror in here.'

'No, Miss Taylor doesn't like hairs in the kitchen. If it wasn't for the mice, she'd get rid of the cat.'

Jessie continued to clear the table. Vera wound small locks of hair into the heated tongs and remarked, 'Why don't you have your hair cut? It's all the fashion to have it shingled and waved.'

'I haven't time to go to the barbers. In any case, I think this style suits me.'

'You must admit, it makes you look very old-fashioned.'

'Some of the men told me I look like Gracie Fields. She has earphones as well.'

'She sings very well, but you wouldn't call her pretty.'

Jessie expected the manageress to share out the duties during the evening meal, but she chatted with Vera about nothing in particular; then suggested that Jessie show her where everything was kept in the bar.

When the shutters were removed, it was obvious that Jock Craig was not impressed by powder and rouge. 'How long is she going to be here?'

'A month.' Jessie glanced across at Vera who was greeting each new arrival correctly, according to rank. She had expected that she would have to show the trainee what to do on her first evening, but Vera knew all the prices and appeared to be familiar with the layout of the bar, so she withdrew to the kitchen.

The arrival of Sergeant Brown changed the course of events. When he came into the kitchen, he exchanged a few polite words with Jessie while she finished dishing up some suppers: he never took liberties and only went into the office by invitation. Vera appeared, but instead of taking the suppers, she said, 'It's your turn in the bar,' and handed back the plates.

When Jessie came for the next order, her assistant was enjoying a chat, but the sergeant was looking ill at ease. As he was too polite to interrupt, he was neither able to advance nor retreat. Seeing his dilemma, Jessie knocked on the office door and informed Miss Taylor of his arrival.

'Oh, is he here? Ask him to come in.'

'Well, it's a bit difficult, I can't get a word in edgeways.'

The manageress came straight to the rescue, so Jessie took the opportunity to return to the bar, where the soldier who had played the 1812 was waiting at the counter. She glanced at the daffodil tucked in the band of his cap.

'Two half pint shandies, please, to celebrate Saint David's Day.'

'I thought you were Irish.'

'No, I come from Ebbw Vale.'

Jessie changed the subject in an effort to hide her ignorance: she thought the leek was the emblem of Wales. 'We had a ton of Welsh nuts delivered yesterday. They're like black diamonds.'

'You can't beat Welsh coal, but it's given my father a dreadful cough and he's still recovering from a fall in the mine.'

'My uncle was burnt to death in a mine in Dysart when he was only nineteen. There was an explosion and four of them were trapped.'

'Was there any compensation?'

'No, the men said it was firedamp. They reckoned it

was a spark from a pick, but the owners said they must have used matches.'

The conversation was interrupted by the arrival of Tug Wilson, who wanted a supper.

Later in the evening, when Jessie was collecting the cups, she came to the table occupied by the two Welshmen. 'You didn't finish telling me what happened.'

'There's nothing else to tell, really, I was four years old and kept crying to see my Uncle Jamie. They lifted me up to let me look in his coffin. He was just like a mummy, all covered in bandages.'

Distracted by the conversation, Jessie had picked up the daffodil and placed it on the tray, then realising her mistake, she said, 'Oh sorry, you want that.'

'Would you like it?'

'Have this one too.' His friend removed the daffodil from his cap.

'Thank you, they'll last several days if I put them in water straight away.'

Jessie carried the tray through to the other side of the counter; Paddy closed the door behind her. 'Thank you, Paddy,' he prompted, because she had not yet acknowledged his courtesy. 'Sure now, it's my pleasure,' he continued and inclined his head as he caught her eye.

At suppertime Vera said she didn't think she'd be able to keep the job as the heat of the kitchen made her feel faint. Miss Taylor hastened to reassure her that cooking wasn't usually part of the general assistant's duties. A simple solution would be that she took over the bar; then she would only have to cook on Jessie's half-day.

The next morning, Jessie jumped out of bed as soon as the alarm clock rang; her roommate didn't move. As she dressed herself, she made more noise than usual, but there was no sign of life in the adjoining bed. Running the tap in the washbasin didn't have the desired effect, so she dropped her shoe with a clatter.

Vera's head appeared. 'There's no point in us both getting up. Be a sport and bring me a cup of tea when you take one to the manageress.' Her head disappeared under the sheet.

Jessie was disgruntled, to say the least: first no cooking and now no stove-cleaning.

Breakfast was ready when the trainee appeared, carrying her empty cup and saucer. 'What was all that banging?' She obviously thought that this was another tactic to disturb her slumbers.

'The soldier on fatigues always kills the cockroaches.'

'Why don't you get some Keating's powder?'

'Miss Taylor has tried everything but the warm, damp heat still brings them.'

During the meal, Vera began to smoke. Miss Taylor was usually more considerate but accepted a cigarette and lit it absentmindedly.

By now, Jessie was undecided about the advantages of having a trainee assistant: she didn't appear to need much training and, so far, she hadn't been of much assistance. However, some of her doubts were dispelled when Vera scrubbed the kitchen floor: she was quick and very thorough. Jessie was slightly upset when Miss Taylor was full of praise, 'Isn't she the one, did you ever see anyone scrub like that?'

However, the kitchen duties could now be carried out at a more leisurely pace. Miss Taylor suggested that Jessie should try her hand at rock cakes. The first batch was slightly burnt on top and doughy inside, but Miss Taylor consoled her that the cakes were edible; next time, the fire must be more carefully stoked to obtain the correct oven heat.

In the evening, Jessie was relegated to the kitchen while Vera took up her newly acquired position in the bar; tripping back and forward to give the orders; then, with perfect timing, calling to collect them. Only once did she fail to arrive, so Jessie carried the plates into the bar. As Vera was serving a corporal at the far end of the counter, she looked across at the tables to find the owners of the fried suppers. A soldier came forward and pointed out that he and his companion had both asked for a slice of bread and a cup of tea.

In the kitchen, Jessie put two slices of bread on one plate and poured two cups of tea.

'Still saving on the washing up, and you with a new assistant,' commented Paddy Riley, who was next but one in the queue. Jessie smiled and looked across at Vera, who was leaning her folded arms on the bar, engrossed in conversation with a corporal.

'What would you like?' The question was addressed to the next customer.

'A cup of tae,' said Paddy Riley. Jessie took no notice and served the first man.

As she walked towards the kitchen, Vera's penetrating voice rang out across the bar. 'Where do you keep the men's hankies, Jessie?'

'In the bottom drawer nearest you, Mrs Shane,' she replied with a quick glance at Paddy Riley, whose nonchalant air belied the fact that he must have heard her name.

As she poured the tea in the kitchen, Jessie pondered that this was the chance Paddy had been waiting for and he was about to tease her mercilessly. She returned to the bar and was relieved to find him alone at the middle of the counter. Jock Craig was concentrating on the billiards and Vera was causing a commotion as she walked around the tables, collecting the cups and joking with the men.

83

Not daring to look up, Jessie placed the cup of tea on the counter.

'Sure now, isn't that the luck of the Irish? First I'm being sent to the end of the queue and now you're ignoring me.' He held his sixpence tightly in his fingertips as he sighed, 'With you being on such familiar terms with a sergeant, I couldn't be expecting you to say a few friendly words to a mere private.'

'Oh, but Sergeant Brown doesn't come to see...' The words tailed off as she realised that he had only made the statement so that she would contradict him. She glanced up and was surprised to find that he wasn't interested in her explanation: his gaze was fixed on the cup and saucer. He ran his fingers through his curly hair, a perplexed wrinkle on his brow; then, after a few seconds, he said, 'What's happened to that?'

'The tea is freshly made.' Jessie presumed he was alluding to the contents of the cup.

'Everyone knows you can't make a dacent cup of tae. No, I mean the cup.'

He picked up the brand new Naafi cup and saucer and inspected it carefully.

'Not a single chip or a crack. Did you forget that one when you were throwing them from the counter to the sink?'

'Och, yi really are terrible, Private Riley!' The tone of her voice conveyed her exasperation, as she took his sixpence.

He was serious when she handed him his change, but there was a mischievous glint in his eye as he put the money straight back in her hand. 'Aren't you making a mistake?'

'No, I don't think so.' She checked that she had given him a three-penny piece and two pennies.

'Wouldn't the tae be a penny extra to pay for the cups?'

84

He cupped his head in his hands and rested his elbows on the counter as he gazed wistfully into her eyes. 'Sure now, if the Naafi goes bankrupt, I won't be able to see my brown-eyed Mavoureen any more.'

Jessie blushed as she held out the three coins, but he didn't take them.

'Go on, say it just once more,' he pleaded.

'Say what?'

'Och, ye really are terrrible, Paddy Riley.' As he rolled his rrr's and imitated her actions, she couldn't help laughing at his mimicry. She turned away and nearly collided with Vera, who had just drawn a pint for Jock Craig. It was obvious from his sullen expression that Jessie had incurred his displeasure with her tête-à-tête.

Vera came to the rescue: 'If you don't mind, lance corporal, what did you get all those ribbons for?'

Jock Craig's frown lifted slightly as he recited the honours he had received in the war. Jessie stopped to listen because her step-father had also been in France until he was discharged with trench feet. Jock Craig pointed to the last ribbon for good conduct. 'And that was for twelve years of –'

'Undetected crime,' said Jessie.

Jock Craig looked up in surprise and gave a chuckle.

'Well, you couldn't be the daughter of a Gordon and not know that one,' she added, as she turned towards the kitchen.

She knew that Paddy would be waiting for her to look round. In return for a smile, she received his usual saucy wink.

Although Sergeant Brown had become a frequent visitor in recent weeks, he declined the invitation to supper that evening. Usually, they had cocoa, but when politely offered tea or coffee, Vera stated her preference for Guinness, adding that she was quite prepared to pay, unless she could have a bottle as her share of the profits. Miss Taylor didn't take exception to the remark and said they could all have Guinness because the staff messing had increased from four to six shillings: three could live as cheaply as two. Jessie said she preferred cocoa, and poured herself a cup while Miss Taylor fetched a Guinness to share with Vera.

The two women started to discuss the advantages and disadvantages of being married. Jessie was surprised when Miss Taylor disclosed that her parents were both dead and she no longer had a home in Ireland. As her sister intended to remain in England, she would also stay here after she was married. Vera pointed out that it was the policy of the Naafi to separate husband and wife by transferring one of them to a different barracks. The conversation held little interest for Jessie, so she wished them both 'Goodnight', and went to bed.

'Are you asleep?'

Jessie opened her eyes. She had been fast asleep but was now wide-awake.

'Be a sport and turn off the light. I stubbed my toe when I was trying to find my way back to bed in the dark last night.'

Jessie did as she was asked.

'Sorry dear, to trouble you, but I can't sleep unless I read a book.'

9

Relegation to the Kitchen

The new assistant was already au fait with the system and quickly adopted her own routine. During the next fortnight, she scrubbed all the floors in rotation. Jessie was very impressed with her speed and efficiency as she went through the canteen like a whirlwind, even remembering to scrub the bars under the kitchen table. Miss Taylor was in a very good humour when Vera volunteered to scrub the floor of the grocery bar, which was normally part of her work.

Jessie had more time to spare and took the opportunity to practise rock cakes, scones, apple tarts, and bacon and egg pie. The manageress was particularly pleased with the latter because all the scraps of bacon from the grocery bar were used up instead of being written off. The baking was not up to Mrs Hadley's high standard but Jessie consoled herself that at least it was better than that of the army cook.

Corporal Smythe had gradually become a nuisance. At first he had requested cigarettes and paid for them; now he came early every Thursday morning to borrow five shillings. To give him his due, he always returned the money as soon as he was paid on Friday, but if Vera found out, she would be sure to tell Miss Taylor.

*   *   *

It was now her assistant's second half-day and Jessie was pleased to return to her former job in the coffee bar. Paddy came to the counter. 'Scottie, I want you a minute.'

'I'm rather busy. It's Mrs Shane's night off.'

'Sure now, you're always busy. Could you not be sparing a minute while I tell you about me being thrown aside like an owld glove?'

Her curiosity aroused, she returned to the counter.

He heaved a sigh. 'Well, was I not thinking I found favour with this girl, when this other fellow comes along and gives her flowers. Now I'm out in the cold, as you might say.'

'Couldn't you manage to give her some flowers?'

'I was thinking that meself, but I'm not sure if she would accept them from an Irishman.'

'I don't see why not.'

'I'm a bit shy, you see.'

So far the story had been plausible, but now her suspicions were aroused.

'Paddy, you're pulling my leg.'

'Would I do a thing like that? In any case, where are my hands and where are your legs?' He was leaning on the counter with his hands tucked behind his elbows.

As Jessie glanced down, he withdrew his right hand and held out a green sprig of shamrock. 'Scottie, I know you prefer daffodils, but isn't it the thought that counts?'

'Where did you get that from?' she asked, to hide her embarrassment.

'Sure now, Mammy wouldn't leave her favourite son without a piece of shamrock on Saint Patrick's Day. She sent it from the owld country to protect me from all these hathens.'

'Thank you, but I must go now,' she said, as she accepted the shamrock.

'Sure now, that's a pity when Taffy is just going to play our record.'

She didn't know what he meant but was determined to end the dalliance.

In the kitchen, Jessie was wiping the table when the strains of 'Are you lonesome tonight, do you miss me tonight?' floated through the entrance to the bar. She started to giggle.

Miss Taylor said grumpily, 'What's the matter with you?'

'It's just something Paddy Riley said.'

'Private Riley, if you don't mind. I might have known it would be some of his old flannel.'

Miss Taylor had been weighing up orders in the grocery bar, but when Sergeant Brown arrived, she came to make a cup of tea. Jessie returned to the bar to drain off the last of the bitter and, as usual, Jock Craig volunteered to put up the new barrel.

Sergeant Brown stayed to supper and was about to depart when there was the click of high heels on the concrete yard. 'Would you mind if I go out through the grocery, Molly?' With two long strides across the corner of the kitchen, he disappeared into the shop, followed by Miss Taylor.

Vera came through the scullery door. 'Was that Sergeant Brown?'

Jessie chose her words carefully. 'Yes, he came to help Miss Taylor lift some of the sacks.' To avoid being subjected to the inquisition, she continued, 'Lance Corporal Craig put up a new barrel tonight. I'll tap it when it's settled. He won't mind having a Whitbread in the mean time.'

Vera wasn't paying attention. Her head was turned on one side, listening for sounds in the grocery bar.

Miss Taylor returned and asked Jessie to fetch a bottle of Guinness; then went to the office to pay the money into the bar float.

The manageress was still locking up when Jessie went to bed.

Throughout her stay, Vera had taken great pains to create a good impression and convince Miss Taylor that she was doing her fair share of the duties. For the sake of harmony, Jessie had pretended not to notice that she only undertook the tasks she preferred.

Tea in bed, the first morning, had set a precedent. When the alarm rang, 'You won't forget my tea, dear,' was repeated with monotonous regularity. Vera remained in bed while Jessie cleaned the range and scoured the kitchen sink to remove the last traces of the cockroaches. By the time her assistant appeared, just after eight, she had usually finished wiping the kitchen table and was in the scullery having a wash. Vera would settle herself beside the range to smoke a cigarette and drink a second cup of tea while she imparted the latest gossip. In the mean time, Jessie would be frying the bacon and laying the table.

The manageress was responsible for cleaning her own room, but Jessie routinely shook the hearthrug in the yard after she cleared the ash from the grate. Vera found great favour when she not only scrubbed the floor of the grocery bar, but also volunteered to wash and polish the office floor. Jessie made no comment when Miss Taylor went into raptures about the shine on her linoleum. She had already noticed that when it was the turn of their room, the lino just inside the door received preferential treatment; the rest of the floor was only wiped with a damp cloth.

As Vera was determined to reduce her weight by chain-smoking, Jessie refused any offers of assistance with the preparation of food. In consequence, she did all the cooking and made the sandwiches while her assistant devoted more time to making herself 'presentable'. Jessie envied her courage as she sauntered across the yard, with her towel tucked under her arm, to avail herself of the facilities in the sergeant's mess: a shower would have been a welcome diversion after a morning over a hot stove.

When the bar opened at midday, Vera would install herself for the first half hour, but when dinner was served, she would take it in turns with Jessie to answer each summons. After the meal, she would excuse herself with an appropriate remark, such as, 'the cups are piled high in the bar. I really must make a start,' which meant that Jessie was left to struggle with the heavy saucepans and greasy roasting tins. Occasionally, she would jump to her feet, saying cheerfully, 'My turn in the scullery, dear,' but this was only after a cold lunch when the cups in the bar outnumbered the few dishes used by the staff. She usually helped to prepare high tea but always made herself scarce as soon as Jessie carried the dishes into the scullery.

At five-thirty, she would re-emerge from the bedroom in a cloud of eau-de-cologne, to trip along the passage, her bouncing bosom half a pace ahead of her high-heeled shoes, which leant outwards under the strain of her weight.

On one particular evening, Jessie was weighing up the ingredients for a batch of rock cakes when she became aware of an altercation in the bar. She couldn't see Jock Craig, but the tone of his voice conveyed the impression that he was tight lipped as he asked to see the manageress. Vera informed him that the manageress was out. The lance corporal replied that this didn't surprise him, since she was never there when she was needed.

Vera's tone was dictatorial. 'You can have a Whitbread when you've paid for that pint. You are going to pay for it, I presume.'

Jock Craig was becoming truculent. 'I'm not in the habit of not paying for anything I have.'

Vera had obviously not been listening when Jessie had explained that the beer hadn't settled. However, the matter could easily be resolved: Jock Craig would not have bothered to taste the cloudy beer, so the pint could be returned to the barrel.

Jessie stepped towards the bar, with the intention of intervening but, by now, Vera had fetched the Whitbread. She kept her hand firmly on the neck of the bottle until the lance corporal added a further sixpence to the coins already on the counter. Only then, did she release her grip and pick up the money. She was about to remove the offending glass, but Jock Craig was too quick for her and placed it out of her reach.

Realising that her assistant wouldn't welcome any interference, Jessie returned to the kitchen.

After a short while, Vera retired to the bedroom, presumably to touch up her face and calm her temper with a cigarette. Jessie took the opportunity to slip into the bar to give the lance corporal a refund. He refused her offer, telling her not to worry, since the matter would be put right when he lodged a complaint with the manageress.

Jessie looked after the bar until Vera reappeared in the kitchen, to relate her version of the incident in a loud voice. 'That miserable Scotsman was looking for a free pint, but he needn't think he can put one over on me. The manageress told me it was only a matter of time before he erupted again. If he's going to pick on me, he'd better think again.'

On her return, Miss Taylor listened sympathetically to the tale of woe. She was already prejudiced and not particularly concerned about the rights and wrongs of the case. 'That man really is incorrigible,' she agreed.

Vera and Miss Taylor were sitting at the table, sharing their cigarettes and drinking Guinness. For once, Jessie was pleased that she wasn't included in the conversation. Vera's handling of the complaint had been partly influenced by the Scotsman's reputation, which Miss Taylor had helped to foster, but she was also resentful that she was obliged to behave with decorum under his watchful eye.

It was no coincidence that Sergeant Brown came to supper on Vera's night off. At first Jessie was puzzled by the conversation.

'You're sure it'll be all right to use your bunkroom, Cyril?'

'Of course, I've made arrangements with Harry. Charlie will have everything he needs.'

'Oh well, that's settled. How about you Jessie? Would you like to go home for the Easter weekend?'

'Oh, yes, thank you,' she replied, without a moment's hesitation.

'Most of the Depot will be away so I can manage. You didn't have much time off when you first arrived. A weekend off will make up for it.'

While Miss Taylor continued to discuss the arrangements for the mysterious Charles, Jessie's thoughts were directed to other matters: her hands, usually reddened by soda in the washing up water, were now chapped by the cold wind. Her recent purchases of glycerine and rosewater, gardening gloves and black stockings had made a hole in her wages. By the time she paid her fare there wouldn't be much left to take home.

Miss Taylor accompanied the sergeant to the back door; then sat down at the table to light a cigarette. 'You quite like Sergeant Brown.'

'Yes, he always includes me in the conversation.'

'Oh, I see.'

'Is your brother coming to see you at Easter?'

'What gave you that idea? I haven't any brothers.'

'Oh, I thought Charles...'

'Charles is my fiancé. He's coming from Bury.'

'But I thought Sergeant Brown...'

'Not at all, Sergeant Brown is engaged to a girl in London. He's going to see her this weekend. Our friendship is purely platonic.'

Jessie picked up the dishes and carried them into the scullery because she didn't know what to say. The manageress and the sergeant made a very handsome couple: he had the bearing of an officer; she was always smart and fashionably dressed. Although he was probably just over thirty, the disparity in their ages was not apparent: they seemed to be a perfect match.

The days flew past. Jessie was giving her bedroom a special clean before Easter when Vera brought her a letter; then lit a cigarette and perched it on the chest of drawers while she powdered her nose. Seeing her roommate's expression, she dusted the fine deposit off the newly polished surface, dropping the ash on the freshly brushed mat. 'Cigarette ash is good for carpets; it keeps the moths away,' she said, then as an afterthought, 'I bet you'll be pleased to see the back of me!'

'No, you've been such a great help with the scrubbing.'

'Only three days to go! I'll be glad to leave this dead and alive hole. I hope the next place will be in a town. With a bit of luck, there might even be a gas ring.'

Jessie started to tear open the envelope.

'Why don't you use make-up? Your face is shining as if it's been polished. What you need is some Pond's vanishing cream.'

Jessie couldn't help being amused, despite the criticism. 'I've just started to use Pear's soap. Miss Taylor said the carbolic made me smell like a hospital, but I can't afford make-up, it's a bit too dear.'

'You want to put in for a transfer. Ask for a place where you don't have to pay railway fares just to go to the pictures.'

Jessie had stopped listening: she had found two one-pound notes inside the letter. The explanation was that Mam had been on the way to place father's bet with the local bookie's runner when she had decided to invest a shilling each way. She rarely had a flutter and apologised for risking her daughter's hard-earned wages, but the horse had romped home at a hundred to one. The outstanding bills were now paid and it was only fair that Jessie should have the remainder of the windfall.

Apart from the various activities of the family, there was one further item of news: one of the canteen girls at Carlisle had mentioned some time ago that she was being transferred to Burscough, but she had developed a bad rash and was now on the sick list. Presumably, Vera had been sent as a substitute for the girl, who was not a trainee, and neither was Vera, for that matter!

10

The Vacation

The great day came at last. Jessie sat in the third-class compartment of the crowded train, happy at the prospect of being reunited with her family. It was only three months since she had left home, but it seemed like years; she had such a lot to tell them. The shrill whistle of the engine startled her. As the train slowed down, she was surprised to find that the station was Carlisle.

At the approach to the castle, Jessie's legs refused to go any faster; when she reached the married quarters, she mounted the stairs two at a time.

Anna heard the footsteps and opened the door of the flat. 'It's Jessie,' she cried.

Mam dried her hands to give her a hug. 'Did you have a good journey?'

'What's the canteen like?' asked Isabel.

'It's a small canteen, only about twenty-four men, all privates and corporals. There are some sergeants, but they don't come into my bar.'

'Now give her a chance to take her coat off,' said Mam, as she filled the kettle.

After tea Anna plied Jessie with questions while Mam continued to scrub the canvas suits. As it was the school holiday, the children were allowed to stay up later, but when Father didn't return from the sergeant's mess, Mam decided they had better not wait up.

Saturday dawned a clear, bright spring day. Mam brought Jessie a cup of tea, wished her a happy birthday and explained that she was going to the grocery to pay the bill with her earnings. Although it was a holiday, Mr Curtis would open, but only for a few hours to oblige the married families.

Jessie had dressed and was starting to lay the table when she returned.

'Mr Curtis is ever so worried, Jessie. There's a G.O.C. inspection next week and the woman who scrubs the place hasn't been for two weeks. He asked me if I could do it, or if I knew anyone. I'd do it for him but I must iron the suits.' She hesitated. 'I don't suppose you would help him out. He'll give you the two weeks' money he would have paid Nellie.'

'Couldn't he scrub it himself?' Jessie inspected her chapped hands, which were just beginning to heal.

'I don't think he's able. He told your father he has a war wound in his back.'

'Surely there's someone else who could do it.'

'I doubt if he'll find anyone as it's holiday weekend. I wish you'd help him out, Jessie, he's such a nice man, and so understanding when I can't pay the bill on time.'

'Oh, all right, I'll do it.'

'That's a good lass. I'm sure your work will be appreciated.'

'I knew you would get round oor Jessie. She's daft to go cleaning on her holiday,' chimed in Anna, who had been listening to the conversation.

'Just you mind your own business. You've got too much to say for yourself. When you start work, next week, you'll learn that a still tongue carries a wise head.'

Anna accepted the rebuke, without comment, but pulled a face as soon as Mam's back was turned. Jessie pretended not to notice and went into the bedroom to

98

change into an old frock before she set out to offer her services.

In response to the doorbell, a thin grey-haired man came through from the back of the grocery. 'What can I do for you?'

'You wanted someone to do some scrubbing.'

He looked Jessie up and down: five feet tall and a mere seven stone four pounds. 'It's very dirty. I need someone strong.' He hesitated. 'All right, if you think you're able. Perhaps you could start in the office.' He went off to find the cleaning materials and Jessie set to work with a will.

The office floor was soon completed and the lino on the shop floor presented no problems, but when Jessie was taken to the rear of the army hut, her heart sank: the packages and boxes under every rack would all have to be pulled out before the floor could be scrubbed. It looked as if the bare boards hadn't seen soap and water for months.

Mam appeared at the entrance just as Jessie came to the conclusion that Anna was right: she must be daft to undertake such a task.

'I came to see how you're getting on. Can I do that last bit for you?'

'No, I'll not be long now. It's not worth your while starting.'

'I can see it's queer and dirty.'

'The path outside is just earth and stones. I suppose the dirt treads in.'

Jessie could hear her mother's voice in the shop as she cleaned the bucket and draped the floor cloth over it. Her shoulders ached; the hems of her frock and petticoat were wet and filthy; the holes in her stockings were hardly noticeable because her knees were so dirty.

When Jessie was ready to leave, Mr Curtis handed her a ten-shilling note. 'That's the money the woman would have received for two weeks' work. I don't know how to thank you. Now, what kind of chocolates would you like?'

Jessie thanked him and said he had paid her quite enough, but her reluctance to accept a gift was not shared by her mother. 'It's your birthday. So far, you've only had a few good wishes. You can't refuse such a kind offer.'

Back at the flat, the family gathered round to admire the present. Anna remarked, 'We should take that box of chocolates to the theatre tonight and hand them round, like the toffs do.'

Mam looked at the clock and consulted the *Cumberland News* to find the advertised programme of Her Majesty's Theatre. It turned out to be the first night of *The Gondoliers*, presented by the Carlisle Choral Society. If Jessie and Anna had their tea straight away, they would be just in time for the performance.

Outside the theatre there was a long queue but, eventually, the sisters were on their way up to the gallery. By ascending the stone steps two at a time, they overtook most of the people who had been ahead of them and collapsed, breathless, on to the front row.

It was not long before the theatre was filled to capacity. The buzz of conversation subsided as the house lights dimmed and the footlights cast a warm glow on the velvet curtains. There was an expectant hush as the leader of the orchestra raised his baton to conduct a continuous cascade of music; the curtains slowly parted to reveal the backdrop of a Piazza in Venice. The audience continued to be entranced by the music and colourful scenes: there wasn't a sound in the auditorium as the comical plot unfolded.

At the interval, the house-lights went up and the bird's eye view of the wealthy people in the stalls was as much part of the entertainment as the opera itself.

During the second act, cigarette smoke drifted in grey wisps across the spotlights; the theatre became hot and stuffy. As there was no backrest, Jessie leaned forward with her elbows on the rail to watch the movement and colour through the haze.

The performance ended with a rapturous ovation, which seemed as if it would go on forever, but the opening bars of the National Anthem brought everyone to their feet, and they remained standing to attention until the end. The gaiety of the music had been infectious and there was a jocular atmosphere as the people struggled into their coats and scrambled for the exits.

Outside the theatre, Jessie's breath turned to vapour, but the warm air, trapped between layers of clothing, prevented her from noticing the chilly evening breeze.

On the way home, Anna kept humming 'Take a Pair of Sparkling Eyes': the audience had warmed to the sentiment of the refrain and had insisted on two encores. Jessie couldn't help wondering if Paddy Riley's description of her eyes was just coincidental. Previously, she hadn't attached any significance to his words.

On Sunday morning, it was daylight when Jessie awoke and looked at the clock: it couldn't possibly be quarter to eleven, but no, it hadn't stopped. She dressed quickly and went into the living room, where Mam was sitting beside a radiant fire, reading a newspaper.

'Why didn't you call me for Mass?'

'When I looked in, you were fast asleep. You must have been tired after all your hard work and it's a long walk to the church.'

Mam was under the impression she had done her a favour, but it was unthinkable that she had missed Mass while on holiday, when she had risen at six-thirty on every cold, frosty Sunday morning to attend the church at Burscough.

The remainder of the day was spent reading the newspapers, while the gramophone played in the flat below. When Anna began to do the Charleston in time to the music, Mam remonstrated, 'Now stop that. It's not fair on the people downstairs.'

'I doot if they can hear, they're making so much noise.'

'Maybe, but we've got to be careful: we are only civilians and they are Borderers.'

'All right, I'll sing some songs instead.'

'You don't sing songs on the Sabbath, only hymns.'

'We're no' in Scotland now, this is England and nobody bothers. That gramophone has been –'

'Now let that be an end to it.'

On Monday, it was decided that Jessie must leave in time to catch the train. Mam had work to do, so the family accompanied Jessie to the station. As they approached the sweet shop, Jamie extracted a halfpenny from his pocket and demanded a poky hat. Jessie would have allowed him to have it, but Anna said it was much too cold for ice cream and yanked him along, ignoring his protests.

At the station, a train driver was polishing his engine. Seeing the small boy, with eyes like saucers, he stopped work and volunteered to lift him into the cab. From down below, his sisters could hear Jamie asking where the coal went. A few seconds later, there was a deafening blast as the engine let off steam.

Jamie was returned, flushed with excitement. He refused to take Anna's hand, clinging tightly to Jessie as she tried to board the train.

'I'm glad I'm starting work next week. We'll no' be able to pass the station now he's been on the engine,' Anna shouted as the train began to steam slowly out of the station. Jamie was struggling to free himself and Jessie wondered how she would persuade him to go home, but no doubt the poky hat would provide sufficient inducement.

11

Stormy Weather

Miss Taylor expressed surprise at Jessie's early return from the short holiday. She was sitting at the kitchen table, talking to a dark-haired young man, who looked very relaxed in his shirtsleeves and open waistcoat. 'This is Corporal Charles Bowen.'

'How do you do?' said the young man, rising to his feet.

'Charles will be leaving soon. There's a fresh pot of tea, so help yourself.'

Jessie hadn't anticipated that the manageress would still be entertaining her fiancé when the coffee bar was due to open in ten minutes.

As Charles put on his silky raincoat, shot with purple and grey, she couldn't help noticing his attire: his brown jacket and waistcoat clashed with his pink shirt, gaudy tie, grey Oxford bags and tan coloured shoes. Either the corporal was colour-blind or he had extremely bad taste. His appearance compared very unfavourably with that of Sergeant Brown: the latter was always neatly dressed in a navy-blue suit and tie, grey shirt and well-polished shoes. In all other respects Charles appeared to be a satisfactory suitor: he was at least two inches taller than Miss Taylor and had a cheerful countenance. It was a pity that he lacked discernment in his dress, but no doubt she would put him to rights after they were married.

The manageress refused Jessie's offer to look after the bar while she accompanied her fiancé to the station, saying that she had work to do, but when he departed, she didn't bother to make the drinks and the menu board offered a few snacks instead of the usual meals. Most of the soldiers were still on holiday, and the few remaining were on duty.

Jessie remained in the kitchen, chatting about her visit to theatre. However, there were times during the conversation when the manageress didn't appear to be listening, as she chain-smoked a whole packet of cigarettes. Jessie broke the silence by commenting that it would be nice to see Sergeant Brown again. To her surprise, Miss Taylor wholeheartedly agreed.

On Tuesday, life was once again hectic. In the evening Jessie was so rushed off her feet that the dirty cups began to pile up on the tables. At the first opportunity, she unbolted the counter and walked swiftly across the bar. Private Crosby was sitting in his customary place, making notes, but as she approached, he glanced up and quickly snapped the book shut. She had often wondered what he was writing, and took the opportunity to enquire as she wiped the table. He grinned broadly. 'Something that's not suitable for little girls to see.' She blushed and retreated in haste with her tray of crockery.

Jessie had just recovered from this faux pas when she was stunned by the news of an even greater calamity. Three soldiers were standing at the counter and one of them remarked, sympathetically, 'You look ever so hot, Scottie.' His comment made her conscious of her flushed cheeks and the beads of perspiration on her forehead.

'Oh well, you won't be quite so busy next week when the new cook arrives. He's supposed to be good, so we might even get some decent food.'

'What will Corporal Smythe do? Will he be the assistant?'

'No, he's been posted elsewhere. He left this morning.'

Jessie's face showed her consternation.

'He didn't owe you money Scottie?'

'Yes, I mean no.'

'How much was it?'

'It wasn't very much. I was warned not to give credit or lend money, so it's my own fault.'

'How much is not very much?'

Jessie tried to appear unconcerned as she replied, 'It was only five shillings.'

The three soldiers produced an assortment of coins. 'We can't have that.'

'Oh no, it was my own fault.'

'We'll settle up and get it back later.'

'No, it's very nice of you. He'll probably send it back by post and then I wouldn't know who to give it to.'

'Hope springs eternal, but not this time, if I know anything,' commented one of the soldiers, gloomily.

On Saturday there were several deliveries, but no post for Jessie.

'You are very anxious to receive a letter. Is something wrong?' enquired the manageress.

Pride wouldn't allow Jessie to admit her foolishness. 'I'm expecting a letter from my sister. She's starting work this week and said she would let me know how she's getting on.'

On Monday, Jessie continued to keep watch for the postman. Each time she looked out of the window, she couldn't help smiling to herself at the antics of Blondie, who was taking advantage of the sunshine by peeling potatoes in the sheltered yard that separated the canteen from the cookhouse. First, he fetched a sack; next, he staggered and swayed as he attempted to carry a very large bowl of water down the two steps at the cookhouse door; finally, he brought a bucket and stool. As he cheerfully prepared the dinner, one day in advance, his whistling determined the speed of his work. Jessie found herself waiting for the short pause as each potato plopped into the bowl of water.

At precisely eleven o'clock, Miss Taylor bolted the door of the grocery bar. Almost immediately, someone tried to turn the handle. Jessie was scrubbing the floor, so she didn't hear what the voice called out, but the reply was loud and clear. 'We close at eleven, open again at two.'

The man tried to converse with the manageress, but she marched into the kitchen.

'That will teach him to be here on time,' she commented, as she walked towards the office.

Jessie could hear the angry voice of the late customer as he walked round the outside of the building, but it was not until he turned the corner that she could hear his defamatory description of canteen staff in general. She put her fingers in her ears to shut out the invective as she looked out of the window at the well-built, middle-aged man, dressed in a spotless white jacket, trousers and apron; swinging his arms as he marched in military fashion towards the cookhouse.

Jessie tiptoed into the passage, to make sure that the office door was almost shut, before she went back to the window, nearest to the larder. She gently pushed the casement open and beckoned to the cook. He glowered across at her and said something that, fortunately, she couldn't hear. Blondie wasn't looking in her direction so she hissed through her teeth to attract his attention. When he turned round, she pointed to the cook and beckoned with crooked finger. A few words were exchanged between them; then the cook strode across. Before he reached the window, Jessie put her finger to her lips and whispered, 'What was it you wanted?'

'Two eggs and some grivy brahnin,' he answered quietly.

Jessie gave him two eggs from the larder. 'What was the other thing you wanted?'

'Grivy brahnin, miss,'

'What?'

'Grivy brahnin, for the dinner.'

Jessie was obviously none the wiser, so he stood on tiptoe to poke his head through the window. 'There it is,' he said, pointing to the bottles that were visible through the open larder door. She pointed to each in turn and glanced round to see his reaction.

'That's it, miss.'

'Och, yi mean gravy browning.' She gave him the bottle.

'Yes, that's right miss, grivy brahnin, I'll bring it straight back.'

At dinner time Jessie was slightly nervous because she wasn't sure if Miss Taylor had heard the cook's voice as he had willed her to find the bottle. When Jessie remarked that she had sold quite a few teas but no sandwiches, the manageress replied that the standard of catering over the way had a considerable effect on their trade.

Promptly, at two o'clock, the new cook and his assistant arrived at the door of the grocery bar. Jessie could hear the manageress saying crisply, 'The rations are on the counter, a sack of potatoes on the floor.'

'I'll have the rations on the scale, if you don't mind miss.'

'But I do mind, I'm very busy.'

'Just the same, I've got to look after the interests of the men. It won't take a second. My assistant will lift the heavy bags for you.'

The manageress had no alternative but to re-weigh the entire order.

The cook's voice was stern. 'Three and three-quarter pounds of margarine, the order says four.'

After each item was weighed, there was a prolonged silence and Jessie deduced that the manageress was rectifying the discrepancies.

By standing beside the kitchen table, Jessie could see the cook, motionless, with his arms folded across his chest as he supervised the proceedings. The only correct item appeared to be the unopened sack of potatoes.

It was not until Blondie had carried all the stores out to the barrow that the cook signed the chit, remarking that in all dealings in future he would expect to see everything weighed.

Miss Taylor came into the kitchen and lit a cigarette. 'Did you hear that?'

'Yes, what do you think he'll do?'

'He can please himself.'

She was obviously perturbed, but trying hard not to show it. She vindicated herself by saying, 'I just can't get fifty-six pounds out of a half hundredweight bag of sugar. There's a loss on everything that has to be weighed. I really don't care if he reports me.'

Whereas the manageress was downcast, the cook was elated. He walked behind the barrow, singing lustily. It was not until a long time afterwards that Jessie learned all the words of his song, but she was soon acquainted with the final words of the refrain, 'Knocked 'em in the Old Kent Road.'

Later that afternoon, the cook returned the eggs and apologised because he couldn't find a small container for the gravy browning. Jessie said that it didn't matter: she rarely used it.

At tea time, Miss Taylor was very subdued. 'Jessie, would you do something to help me?'

'Yes certainly.'

'I just can't get the stock right unless I give slightly short weight. There's very little allowance for flour that sticks in the seams of sacks, or for bags that split in transit. I have a problem with almost everything I stock. There's not much I can do about it. I would be grateful if you would help me out.'

Jessie was puzzled because she had only served in the grocery on one occasion.

The manageress continued, 'If you could help by making extra tea, your profits would be up, and then it wouldn't matter if I charged you for a carton of cigarettes you didn't have.'

'But I would need extra sugar and milk to do that.'

'I could easily spare some out of the staff messing.'

'But wouldn't that make my stock wrong?'

'That would be my problem, not yours.'

Jessie was worried about the arrangement, partly because she thought the men would complain about the tea, also because it didn't sound quite honest. Miss Taylor explained that stealing was taking something for yourself, and the whole point of the exercise was to ensure that the Naafi would make the required amount of profit. When Jessie agreed to make the extra tea, the manageress said it would be helpful if she remembered to put the last of the old beer barrel into the new one. Jessie also had doubts about this because she knew that if old milk was put into new, the mixture quickly turned sour. Again she was assured that beer was different; no harm would be done if too much time were not allowed to elapse. As the manageress had far more knowledge and experience, Jessie agreed to carry out her instructions, even if she was not entirely happy.

*   *   *

111

The Area Manager had given the impression that several trainee assistants would be sent to the Depot, but they didn't materialise. The next morning, Jessie tumbled out of bed and was soon dressed, ready for the toils of the day.

In the kitchen, it was almost daylight as Jessie spread newspapers in front of the range and collected the basket of brushes and rags from the larder. The first job was to dismantle the top of the range and brush each oblong plate before it was placed on the newspaper. She was carefully scraping the soot out of the flues when there was a tap on the window. Out of the corner of her eye, she could see the cook's white suit but, once bitten, twice shy; she decided to take no notice. But supposing he needed something for the men's breakfast? The solution was to be firm: no credit, no loans, no serving after hours. Determined to make a stand, she walked across the kitchen and pushed open the casement. To her amazement, an arm came through the window and held out a large white mug. 'A cup of tea, miss, no sugar in it.'

Jessie was so astounded that the white figure was halfway across the yard before she had recovered enough to say, 'Thank you.'

When, later that morning, the cook came to collect the mug, she told him that it was the best tea she had ever tasted, a real treat.

'Good, I'm glad yer enjoyed it, miss,' he replied, and turned to walk away.

'Excuse me, what is your name? My name is Jessie.'

He half turned. 'Stormy, miss, and if that old biddy gives me any more of 'er Gawd almighty cheek, there'll be some very stormy weather round these parts.'

12

Tripping the Light Fantastic

The arrival of the cockney cook made a tremendous difference to Jessie's workload. As the pace in the evenings was now comparatively leisurely, she spent more time in the bar, observing the pastimes of the soldiers as they sat quietly at the tables playing crib, shove halfpenny, dominoes and cards.

Taffy usually provided musical entertainment by playing his records on the hand-wound gramophone. When the rhythm was particularly lively, Chalky would borrow two dessertspoons and play them on every part of his anatomy. Whenever Corporal Graves came into the bar, he always sat at the piano. The arm of the gramophone would immediately be lifted to allow him to warm up with 'A Life on the Ocean Wave'. The men appreciated his remarkable talent: he played a medley, ranging from the classics to the latest hits, without sheet music. Taffy would come to the counter to protest that when the spindle was turning, lifting the needle scratched the record, but he soon forgot his grievance when the corporal played a selection from the operas of Gilbert and Sullivan.

Occasionally, Corporal 'Sausage Sandwich' Harris would try to teach Jessie to speak properly. If she happened to say a phrase the Scottish way, he would kindly correct her. 'No, no, no, Scottie, the crust is no' a wee bit burrned, it's slightly burnt.' His pronunciation was very clear, but it was difficult to say cherch instead of churrch and houzes rather than housses. The soldiers would laugh; even Jock Craig took the lessons in good part.

Jessie was now on friendly terms with Miss Taylor, but in the bar she continued to conduct herself with propriety. When she went out to collect the cups, she replied when the men spoke to her, but didn't stand and chat. Occasionally, she was included in the conversation because there was something of special interest. When Sparks made a crystal set, she was invited to listen to a broadcast from London. She looked doubtfully at the glass cylinder, supported by a piece of wood, but when he gave her an earphone and twiddled with the cat's whisker, she was amazed that she could hear music, played by a dance band.

Paddy Riley usually came in just before closing time, unless he had nothing better to do, in which case he would arrive earlier and sit at one of the tables, chatting to his friends about their work. Most times he would ask for tea and iced cakes and pay for them politely, but when he was with either Blondie or Stan, Jessie prepared herself for the repartee.

Blondie was Swedish. It would have been easy to guess that he was of Scandinavian origin by his fair complexion, blue eyes and high forehead. His flawless English accent gave the impression that he had spent some time in Britain before he enlisted for the RAOC. He enjoyed Paddy Riley's company, despite the fact that he, himself, was more serious and was often puzzled when Jessie didn't take offence at the Irishman's remarks.

Stan Eccles had the broadest accent of all the soldiers at the Depot and was proud to be born in Lancashire. He was also handsome in a different way: his dark, wavy hair and deep brown eyes provided a sharp contrast to his fair skin. Jessie soon became accustomed to his

114

disparaging remarks about his usual topic of conversation: the menu.

When Jessie used the tea bag to make an extra half-gallon, for the first time, she was expecting a derogatory comment and didn't have long to wait.

'Hello, what's happened to the tae, Scottie?' Paddy inspected the pale-coloured brew.

'Nothing.'

'But there's definitely something different about it.'

'I don't think so.'

'Sure now, when I put the spoon in the cup, it doesn't stand up by itself.'

'Are you trying to tell me the tea is too weak, Private Riley?'

'No, it's usually too strong.'

'Then why are you complaining?'

'Now what gave you that idea?'

'I thought you said there was something wrong with the tea.'

'Sure I did not. Blondie, did I say there was something wrong with the tae?'

'Well what did you say?'

'I said it was different.'

'How do you mean, different?'

'You haven't made it as you usually do.'

'In what way?'

'It's drinkable for a change. In fact it's almost possible to taste the sugar.'

Jessie tried hard not to say, 'Och, yi'r terrible, Private Riley.'

'Now tell me what I really want to know.'

'What's that?'

'Are you going to trip the light fantastic with me on Friday, Scottie?'

'What do you mean?'

115

'There's a dance in the village on Friday evening,' said Blondie.

'Oh, but the bar doesn't close until nine-thirty and I'm never finished before ten.'

'That's just an excuse. Sure now, the dance won't finish until two.'

'That's very late and I have to be up early in the morning.'

'Did you ever get the feeling that you're not wanted, Blondie?' Paddy winked at Jessie and carried his tea to a table.

Up to now, it had been out of the question for Jessie to go to a dance because there was too much to do after the bar closed. When Private Winters also asked her if she would be there, she started to seriously consider the possibility. As most of the men would be at the village hall, trade would be even slacker than it had been recently.

Sergeant Brown was sitting in one of the office armchairs, Miss Taylor in the other, when Jessie made her request. The manageress hesitated before giving her consent, 'Only if you leave everything as it should be before you go.'

'Yes, I will. I promise.'

The rest of the week passed quickly. On Friday evening, Jessie surprised herself with her own speed and efficiency: she had managed to finish all the clearing up by ten o'clock.

In the bedroom, she changed into her brown serge dress; then went to the office to take her leave. Miss Taylor said, 'When you come back, knock on my window and I'll let you in. I'm not sitting up until two in the morning though. And don't forget, no hanging about outside to say goodnight.'

'No, I won't. I'll come straight back.'

Jessie hesitated. 'Wouldn't it be easier if I took the key of the scullery door?'

'And pray, how are we going to get out if you lock the door and take the key?'

'I thought Sergeant Brown could go out through the grocery bar.'

'And I suppose I'm expected to make a quick detour in my dressing gown if I want to pay a call in the yard!'

Sergeant Brown said, 'Really, Molly, you should have another key cut.'

'Why should I pay for keys so the staff can lose them?'

The road outside the Depot gates was dark. Jessie stood irresolute, listening to the eerie sound of the leaves rustling in the trees. She tried to convince herself that the noises were just a figment of her imagination. If she ran, she wouldn't hear them.

Out of breath, she arrived at the lighted entrance to the village hall where the sound of music revived her spirits. Inside the porch, a man took her shilling and directed her to a small room where an elderly woman exchanged her coat for a ticket.

With some trepidation, Jessie pushed open the swing doors. The orchestra, consisting of a piano, concertina and a set of drums, was at the far end of the hall, playing a foxtrot. She scarcely recognised the men from the Depot in their civvies as they glided across the floor like professional ballroom dancers.

Making her way through the group of village lads, clustered inside the door, she joined a row of girls, seated along the side of the hall. Most of them wore pretty dresses of taffeta and shot silk, with dancing shoes to match; she began to feel ill at ease in her brown serge.

Some of the men from the Depot came across the hall, but she refused their offers to partner her, without mentioning that her repertoire consisted only of the

Viennese Waltz, Gay Gordon's and Dashing White Sergeant. As soon as the orchestra struck up the 'Blue Danube', one of the village boys whisked her to her feet and shuffled her round the floor, making no apology for treading on her toes. When he asked her to save him the last waltz, she decided that it was time to retrieve her coat and run back along the lonely road to the barracks.

At first there was no reply when Jessie knocked on the window. It was obvious that Miss Taylor had dozed off in the armchair. When she finally opened the back door she said, 'Did the dance finish early?'

'No, I don't like stopping out late.'

By now, the manageress was very cordial. 'There's some milk in the larder; make yourself a cup of cocoa.'

The fire was low and Jessie was too tired to bother.

The bell kept ringing. Jessie groped in the dark for the clock. It was several seconds before she remembered that she had deliberately put it out of reach on the chest of drawers. As she sat on her bed, the cold air failed to revive her and her eyes closed. The sudden forward jerk of her head brought her to her senses; splashing cold water on her face helped to sharpen her wits. As she made her way wearily to the kitchen, she decided there would be no more late night visits to the village hall.

The drudgery of the kitchen made the morning pass slowly. It was Miss Taylor's half-day and, usually, Jessie took the opportunity to have a wash, but not that day: she fell into bed in a state of exhaustion and would have remained there if the alarm clock had not roused her.

In the bar, Jock Craig was waiting for his first pint. 'On your own again?'

'I'm not bothered now. Since the new cook arrived, the supper trade's been very light.'

Paddy was the next to arrive on the scene. 'Hello, Scottie, did you enjoy the dance?'

'I didn't see you, there, Private Riley.'

'Sure now, you said you weren't going – or were you just giving me the slip?'

'I decided to go at the last minute; it was almost over when I arrived.'

Paddy remained at the counter. In between serving customers, Jessie chatted to him about the socials and whist drives organised by the parish priest to keep teenagers off the streets of Aberdeen.

'The Scots played cards on Sunday. Whoever heard the like?'

'Yes, I won quite a few prizes.'

'I won't be playing with you, if I'm a wise man. I was after thinking that you're a quiet home-loving girl and you out dancing on week nights and gambling on Sundays!'

Jessie hastened to correct him. 'No, I can't dance; I mean, not modern dances. I only wish I could.'

'Sure now, you could have lessons at Southport on Tuesdays and Thursdays.'

'Wednesday is my half-day and it wouldn't be convenient to change.'

'I don't suppose it would. Most of us go to sports on Wednesday afternoons so Molly only has to pull one pint for the corporal. She wouldn't be wanting to change the system, would she now?' Then he asked casually, 'Did you ever hear from Smythe?'

'No, I've said goodbye to my five shillings.'

'That's tough luck, I really am sorry.'

It was unusual to have a serious conversation with Paddy, but Jessie was tired after the dance and he could see she was in no mood for frivolity.

* * *

119

The following evening, Paddy arrived just after opening time, accompanied by Stan and Pompey, who perused the menu board.

'Braised onions and butter beans are always on the menu. It's about time someone ate them up. Scottie, when are we going to have some real food like Lancashire Hotpot, 'tato pie or a nice piece of silver hake?' enquired Stan.

'We only have a coal-fired range. It doesn't allow much scope.'

Pompey placed an order for bacon, eggs and tomatoes and the others followed suit.

Jessie cooked the suppers and returned to the bar, where Paddy was leaning on the counter, stirring his tea. This always amused her because the sugar was added to the jug at the same time as the milk and was all completely dissolved.

Pompey studied the plate. 'That looks very tasty. The other girl, Florrie, said she wasn't allowed to serve bacon and eggs ... but still, ours not to reason why, only to do or...' He shrugged as he turned to walk away.

Paddy returned to the subject of the menu. 'Sure now, I've been puzzled many times about that board. Every time a fresh item appears, it tops the list, but what happens when it gets down to fourth place in the league?'

'Well, I'll tell you, but only if you keep it a secret.'

'Cross my heart and hope to ... sure now, I mustn't say that, it's Pompey's line.'

'Well, after the first day, if there's no sale, we have it for our lunch. I still leave it in second place on the board to fill up the space.'

'Camouflage, as you might say.'

Jessie giggled and continued, 'You should have come earlier if you wanted rissoles or meat puddings. They were sold out at the beginning of the evening.'

There was a look of amazement on Paddy's face as he

looked at the clock, then around the empty bar. 'But you've only just opened.'

Jessie continued without the faintest glimmer of a smile, 'That leaves the sausages and pork chops. They are fresh today.'

Sergeant Baxter came to the counter. 'Miss, could I trouble you for a supper?'

Jessie liked the tall, fair-haired sergeant, who was very polite and never failed to return the crockery to the counter. 'How about a nice pork chop with apple sauce?' She looked straight up at him because she dare not catch Paddy's eye.

'Fine.'

When the sergeant had finished his supper, he sat at the table, drinking his tea, and called out laughingly, 'Miss, you're a very good cook, I'd ask you to marry me, if only you were nine inches taller!'

'That's easily remedied, Sarge,' said Tug, 'I'll knock you up a pair of stilts tomorrow.'

Paddy said, 'Now you know that Molly wouldn't allow it, the spoilsport that she is. Wouldn't she be finding some impediment in the Naafi regulations. Doesn't she know them off by heart!'

At that moment Sparks came over to peruse the board.

Paddy said, 'Which supper aren't you going to have? Why not try the smoked salmon, or tripe and onions?'

Sparks was used to Paddy's skylarking and took no notice.

'It's no use looking at that, Sparks.'

For a moment, Jessie thought he was going to disclose the secret, but Paddy leaned across the counter as if to impart some confidential information. 'Sparks can't read, but he doesn't like anyone to know.'

'I think I'll have bacon and eggs,' said Sparks with a grin.

'Didn't I just tell you? Bacon and eggs aren't mentioned on the board.'

After Sparks had been served, there were no other customers. Paddy leaned his elbows on the counter and rested his head in his cupped hands. 'There's still one thing that puzzles me.'

'What's that?'

'Why don't you write up Lancashire Hotpot, 'tato pie and Silver Hake?'

'What good would that do?'

'Under your system, Stan wouldn't get any, but wouldn't it make him very happy to know that his favourite foods were so popular?'

13

Money Matters

On Wednesday morning, Jessie rushed around and completed all the chores in record time. She had already made up her mind to pay her first visit to Orsmkirk.

The sun was shining when she set out, but as the train steamed through the countryside, the wind brought the dark clouds scudding across the sky. By the time she had travelled the short distance to the next station along the line, the sky was completely overcast.

Ormskirk turned out to be a small market town. The shopping centre afforded little protection from the elements and there were no department stores in which to browse. Jessie had expected that there would be a cinema or a theatre, but there didn't appear to be either. As hailstones began to bounce off her gabardine, the delicious smell of freshly baked bread drew her attention to a small shop, which would provide an inexpensive refuge.

A grey-haired lady came through from the back parlour.

'What are those pies on the side?' Jessie enquired.

''Tato pies.'

'May I have two please?'

The lady placed the pies in a bag; then, looking out at the inclement weather, suggested that it would be a good idea to wait for a few minutes until the rain eased off.

With her purchase carefully wrapped in brown paper, Jessie once again set out to explore the town centre. The reflection of her sodden hat in the shop windows convinced her that it would be foolish to linger, but it was too early to return to the canteen. She couldn't think of any other way of passing the time, except by squandering her wages on the fare to Southport.

On the way to the station, she stopped to admire a brown, fitted coat on display in the window of a small draper's shop, but the price of four guineas was far in excess of her savings. Her mother had said in her last letter that she was managing much better now that Anna was a wage earner and not to send any more money. Perhaps she could pay a deposit? 'No credit, no lending money,' Miss Taylor's words rang in her ears.

During the rest of the return journey, Jessie's thoughts kept returning to the coat, but she was more in need of a pair of shoes: her second best ones were down at the heel and scuffed on the toes.

The back door squeaked, despite Jessie's efforts to open it quietly.

Miss Taylor appeared at the scullery door. 'I wondered who was coming in. You're becoming quite attached to the Depot. Back early from the dance, and again today.'

'There were large hailstones at Ormskirk.'

'I've told you before to take my umbrella.'

'But you might need it.'

'Don't be silly. How can I use it when I'm working?'

In the bedroom Jessie changed out of her wet clothes. Before she had time to consider what to do with the pies, Sergeant Brown called her for a cup of tea.

As Jessie sat down beside the kitchen range, he asked, 'Did you say you went to Ormskirk?'

'Yes, but I didn't see much of the town.'

'Didn't you buy anything?' enquired the manageress.

'I saw a lovely coat in a shop window but it was four guineas.'

'Surely you've saved that much by now. You don't spend anything.'

'I expect she's saving up for her holidays,' said the sergeant kindly. 'When's your holiday Molly?'

'I've booked the third week in June. Whether I'll get it is another matter. There's never a relief manageress available.'

'Why don't you train Jessie to take your place? You might find it easier to get a general assistant.'

Jessie said quickly, 'Oh, I don't think I could do Miss Taylor's job. I'm not clever enough to do all that bookkeeping and accounts.'

Sergeant Brown thought for a minute. 'June, yes, I could easily help you with them.'

After the sergeant took his leave, Miss Taylor was deliberating as she smoked her cigarette. 'You know, I think Cyril's right. When the next trainee arrives, she can do the coffee bar and the cooking. That would give you time to learn the grocery bar.'

'Oh but...'

'Oh but nothing, you don't want to remain a general assistant all your life.'

'No but...'

'Apart from anything else, your money will go up to twenty-one shillings if you become a charge hand.'

Twenty-one shillings a week: it wouldn't take long to save up for a coat at that rate.

Miss Taylor read her thoughts. 'How much did you say that coat was at Ormskirk?'

'Four guineas.'

'Why don't you buy it?'

'I've only managed to save two pounds since Easter.'

'I save ten shillings a week out of my twenty-five. I'll draw the money out of the post office for you, then if I deduct seven and six a week off your wages, the money will be paid back well before I need it for my holiday.'

'Oh, I couldn't do that.'

'You're very welcome to borrow it.'

'It's very kind but I don't think I should get into debt.'

'Well, please yourself.'

As Miss Taylor was in a good humour, Jessie decided to risk her derision. 'Oh, I nearly forgot, I had to shelter from the rain at Ormskirk, so I went into a shop and bought some 'tato pies.' She fetched the parcel from the bedroom and unwrapped it.

'Just look at the size of them! We'll never get through them in a month of Sundays.'

'Private Eccles is always asking for 'tato pie; I thought he could have one to use them up.'

'And how much profit are you hoping to make?'

'Oh, I wasn't going to charge him. It's just a joke. He's always teasing me about not having 'tato pie on the menu.'

The following day Miss Taylor expressed her approval when they shared the pie at tea time, and said she might order some from the bakery. When Jessie presented Stan with the local delicacy, Paddy accused her of favouritism, but that was only to be expected. Miss Taylor was hovering near the door of the grocery bar when she returned to the kitchen and said, expectantly, 'Did he ask you then?'

'Ask me what?'

'To go out with him, of course. That was why you gave him the pie, wasn't it?

Jessie's protestations fell on deaf ears; the manageress refused to accept that she had no ulterior motive. Her incredulity was very apparent when she related the episode to Sergeant Brown. 'I've never known a girl like her, Cyril, she doesn't smoke and doesn't drink and doesn't swear and she's never had a boyfriend. Nineteen and never had a boyfriend, could you credit that?'

'Don't tease her, Molly,' said the sergeant, 'there's plenty of time yet.'

The days slipped past and Jessie's scruples about the extra tea were soon dispelled when another stock-taking proved correct. The intermission was brief and her qualms returned when Jock Craig tasted the adulterated beer and said, 'Have you done anything to that new barrel?'

'No,' she replied, but her face was scarlet.

'Then it should go back to the brewers. It's slightly soured.'

'I'll tell Miss Taylor about it.'

Panic stricken, Jessie reported the catastrophe, but the manageress was unconcerned.

'Leave it and see if he complains again.'

The worry of the soured firkin caused Jessie many sleepless nights. However, her prayers were answered when Jock Craig drank only Whitbreads, and the advent of warm weather caused the men to drink shandies, with no further complaints. She continued to doctor the tea, but decided not to mention that she was no longer salvaging the dregs from the previous beer barrel.

Miss Taylor continued to be fanatical about waste of any kind and was annoyed when she had to forego her half-day because a bluebottle had laid eggs on a side of bacon. She inspected each bone in turn, removing any meat that was suspect before she doused it with vinegar. 'What wouldn't I give to be married and not have all the worries of the grocery bar,' she sighed, and sent Jessie to fetch the flypapers from her desk, to replace those over the window.

Jessie's initiation into the higher mathematics of bookkeeping had unravelled some of the mysteries of surplus and nett. She was relieved when she found that two or three pints of beer were still being written off when each barrel was discarded, so any losses were accounted for. The meals and beverages, served in the coffee bar, were expected to yield one hundred per cent profit, but allowance was made for any item which was not consumed. She couldn't understand why Miss Taylor still maintained that if anything had to be thrown away, the stock would be down.

To keep the perishable foods cool and tightly covered with muslin, Jessie had to walk backwards and forwards to the marble shelf in the larder and noticed the unusual happenings across the way. First, trestle tables and benches were spread out in the yard; then two young men, armed with scrubbing brushes, set to work to scour the white wood. On another day, the baking tins, coated with black deposits of burnt fat, were stacked outside the cookhouse door and Jessie presumed there was going to be a new issue. Catching sight of her at the window, Stormy stopped singing 'Any Old Iron', and crossed the yard. 'Pass your tins out, miss. Blondie will clean them for you.'

'Thank you, Stormy, but I daren't. She would be the first to find out.'

Afterwards, Jessie regretted that she hadn't risked Miss Taylor's wrath: treated with caustic, the cookhouse tins sparkled like silver, while the canteen tins resisted all her efforts to clean them with scouring powder and elbow-grease.

14

The Price of Honour

Apart from a few soldiers left on duty, the Depot was deserted during the Whitsun weekend. On Saturday afternoon Jessie sat at the kitchen table, trying to compose a letter to her mother, but it was difficult to concentrate. She was gazing out of the window at the cloudless blue sky when Stormy came out of the cookhouse and strode across the yard.

'What are you doing, miss?'

'Trying to write a letter.'

'Care to come and inspect my cookhouse, miss?'

Jessie was delighted with the invitation.

'Good, whenever yer ready, miss.'

She quickly made up the fire and checked that all the doors were locked.

Pompey opened the cookhouse door. 'Come in, Scottie,' he said, standing to attention, as if she were a guest of honour.

Stormy had good reason to be proud of his spotless kitchen. He explained the intricacies of his newly acquired stove, on which the brass fittings gleamed, then Jessie was taken on a conducted tour of the rest of the cookhouse.

'Care for a cup of tea, miss?' The cook waved a finger at the four soldiers, seated on a form. 'You blokes move along and make room for the lidy.' On the table in front of her he placed an enamel plate and a knife, 'hall-marked' with the army crest; then he offered her a piece of flaky pastry, spread with marmalade, and served it with a mug of tea. 'Everything all right, miss?'

'Yes thank you, Stormy, the pastry is delicious.'

'I expect yer make good pastry, miss.'

'I haven't had much time to practise.'

'How many hours do yer work, miss?'

'I don't know; I've never bothered to count.'

'We reckon you work eighty a week.'

'I quite like my work. The men in the bar are good company.'

'It strikes me, that old biddy is always aht, and when she's not, that la-de-da sergeant's in.'

'The sergeant helps her to do the books.'

'Oh yers. I've walked past the winder in the evening when she's bin sittin' on 'is knee, 'avin' a bit of the old 'ows yer farver!'

Pompey frowned at Stormy, so he returned to the original subject.

'Does yer old man know how many hours you work?'

'No.'

'Do yer mind telling me how much they pay yer?'

'Fifteen shillings a week, but there's sixpence off for insurance.'

'Cor blimey, if me daughter had to work all those hours for fourteen and a tanner, I'd blow me bloody top – if you'll pardon the expression miss.' The fleeting thought caused his sanguine cheeks to puff up, and his fearsome brows to knit together. It crossed Jessie's mind that he was old enough to be her father.

'Oh, but I get board and lodging as well.'

'And I'll bet that ain't much. You write and tell yer old man how much yer get.'

'The trouble is, there's no work in Carlisle. I'd rather be here than unemployed. In any case, since you came it's much easier, the men don't want so many suppers.'

'I still think it's bloody ridiculous. Eighty hours for fourteen bob a week.'

'It's much better than being in service. I meet lots of people.'

'And that's another thing; yer don't lock that back door at night.'

The cook looked surprised when Jessie started to laugh, so she related the tale of how she had locked Miss Taylor out.

'Serve her right. Yer should do it again some time and then she'd remember 'er key.'

Thereby hung another tale, but it wasn't good policy to tell it: the cook was already incensed at the shortcomings of her superior.

The time had passed quickly and the kitchen fire would have to be refuelled or the kettles would take too long to boil. Jessie thanked Stormy for his hospitality and returned to the canteen.

In the evening Jock Craig was first in the bar, as usual. 'I hear you went to tea in the cookhouse. You were honoured.'

'Yes, Stormy's kitchen is spotless. He puts us to shame.'

'Different to that old scrounger, we were all pleased to see the back of him.'

As they chatted, Jessie was watching Pompey, Tug and Nobby, who were having a discussion as they sat at a table. Tug kept shuffling a pack of cards.

Pompey said, 'Go on, you ask her.'

Jessie wondered what they wanted, but it was bad manners to eavesdrop, so she returned to the kitchen. There was a rap on the counter: the three men were waiting for tea and cakes. After she had served them, there was nothing else to do, so she chatted with Jock about the latest gramophone records.

'Scottie,' Pompey sounded rather diffident.

'Yes, can I get you something?'

'As you aren't very busy, we wondered if you'd play Newmarket. You see, we need four players.'

'I've never played Newmarket.'

'Don't worry, we'll show you what to do.'

'What if I have some customers?'

'We'll dash round and serve them for you.'

Jessie didn't require any further persuasion. Tug brought the cards to the counter; Pompey pushed a pile of coppers towards her.

'There's your stake money, Scottie. We're playing for half-pennies.'

'Just a minute, I've got some money.'

'Don't bother Scottie, you can use this.'

'I won't be a minute,' she insisted. She fetched a shilling from her bedroom, which they exchanged for coppers.

By the time Paddy Riley arrived, they had played several games. Jessie was collecting up her coppers before she went off to cook the suppers.

'I see Molly is out tonight.'

Jessie didn't answer because the back door was unlocked and Stormy's warning had made her more cautious: anyone could make off with the office float while she was serving in the bar.

'Sure now, I don't know what Molly would say if she knew all her staff were playing cards.'

'All her staff?'

'Well, where's the cook, the tea girl and the washer up?'

Jessie laughed and was about to fetch his cup of tea when he turned to the trio.

'How much have you lost, lads?'

'I'm winning,' said Pompey.

'That's what happens when you play with sharpers. They let you win the first time and fleece you the next.'

'Scottie lost two pence.'

'Now I'm surprised at that, with her being the Scottish champion.'

'Really?' said Pompey.

'Wasn't she after telling me, herself, that she'd won more than her fair share of prizes.'

'That was for whist,' said Jessie.

'The lance corporal there, now he's a wise man, he wouldn't play with her.'

To everyone's surprise, Jock Craig nodded and said, 'Aye yir recht, noo jist mind whit yir da'en lads or she'll tak the breeks aff the lot o' yi.'

Paddy and the trio were flabbergasted: the anglicised Scotsman had never previously lapsed into his native tongue. Jessie was too embarrassed to explain that, in Scotland, it is customary to lose your trousers, not your shirt. However, her quick thinking rescued her. 'Aye, they dinna ken, the best laid schemes o' mice and men gang aft aglae.'

Paddy was only temporarily lost for words. 'Sure now, the country's being invaded by foreigners.'

When the bar closed, Jessie sat pondering on the day's events while awaiting the return of the manageress. To pass the time, she jotted down the number of hours she worked and came to the conclusion that Stormy was wrong: he made it eighty hours; she only made it seventy-one and a half. The sound of the back door put an end to her calculations, but as they drank their cocoa, Miss Taylor asked, 'What are all those figures on the cover of your writing pad?'

'Oh, I was just working out how many hours I work.'

'And what in heaven's name put that into your head? And how many hours do you work?'

'About seventy.'

And whose fault is that, may I ask? Florrie was always cleared up by two o'clock every day. When she put the shutters up, she'd finished for the night.'

'Oh I'm not complaining, I was just amusing myself to pass the time.'

On Sunday morning the manageress was pensive when she received her morning tea.

Jessie returned from Mass to find their breakfast ready and a very affable Miss Taylor, who suggested that she should take the evening off. She politely turned down the offer: there wasn't much to do in Southport on Sundays.

As she went out at five o'clock, Miss Taylor commented that it was Jessie's own fault if she didn't accept the time when it was given.

Tug, Pompey and Nobby were in the coffee bar when Jessie took down the shutters. Her first impulse was to refuse when they asked her to join them in another game of Newmarket, but, on second thoughts, she had been offered free time, so she was entitled to please herself. She retrieved her little bag of coppers from under the counter and they started to play.

Several games were won and lost; then one game ran on for some time. The kitty began to mount up; the coppers were changed to silver. Jessie had used up all her money and would have withdrawn, but Pompey said she couldn't give up now and shared his coppers with her.

Once again the cards were dealt. In her hand Jessie had four of the same suit and the three of spades. 'Can I buy?' she asked, putting down a halfpenny and picking up the ten of hearts.

Tug said, 'I can go three.'

Pompey said, 'Four and clubs are trumps.'

Tentatively, Jessie said, 'I think I can go five.'

'Go ahead, Scottie, what are trumps?'

'Hearts,' she said with conviction: she knew that was right. She put down the ace; Nobby played the two; Pompey a seven and Tug put down a spade. Jessie played the King and kept careful watch as the others selected their cards and placed them on the counter. When she played the Queen, the others quickly threw out an assortment of cards. The next highest card was the Jack; she decided to play it first, and followed it with the ten. The others were convulsed with laughter.

Nobby rocked with mirth and said, 'That's not the way to play cards Scottie.'

'Oh, what did I do wrong?'

He picked up the five tricks she had taken. 'That's what you call a running flush Scottie. You don't play it, you put it down and say, beat that if you can.'

'Oh, I didn't know that.'

Tug was still laughing. ' "I think I can go five!" '

Pompey started to push the kitty towards her. 'That's yours, Scottie.'

'I couldn't take all that.'

'Actually, Scottie, I'm starving, could you rustle up some bacon and eggs?'

At that moment, Paddy came into the bar, strolled up to the counter and looked from one to the other.

'You warned us to be careful, Pat. Scottie's just won the kitty.'

Paddy smiled across at Jessie. 'Sure, if you'll pour me a nice cup of tae, with a spoonful of sugar, I promise not to reveal the disgraceful happenings in the men's mess.'

'That's a deal.'

Paddy shook his head in mock reproach. 'Sure we're even talking in gambling terms now.'

135

During the days that followed, Jessie made several attempts to arrange another game of Newmarket, but each time she tried to bring up the subject, the trio who had lost their money were always rushing off somewhere, or playing billiards, or too tired to concentrate.

A fortnight elapsed and Jessie was worried in case Miss Taylor would discover the bag of coppers under the counter. She attempted to enlist the help of Jock Craig. 'I've tried to arrange another game but they're always full of excuses. Would you give them their money back for me?'

'No, they would be very offended.'

'But it was seven and sixpence. They can't afford to lose all that.'

'If they weren't prepared to lose, they shouldn't gamble.'

'But I can't take all that.'

Jock shrugged. 'Would you have been upset if you'd lost?'

'No.'

'Well you should be pleased you won – so stop worrying yourself.'

Jessie couldn't let the matter rest there. A few evenings later, when Jock was alone in the bar, she returned to the subject. 'My mother would be upset if she knew I'd taken money off complete strangers.'

Jock Craig smiled. 'The RAOC is a very proud regiment. In this Depot we have some of the finest men in the land.'

'Oh, yes,' she said quickly, because she didn't want him to think she doubted the integrity of his comrades.

He ignored her interruption and continued, laconically, 'It is their considered opinion that the honour of the regiment is worth more than a dollar – so dinna worry yir bonnie heed lassie.'

15

Crisis in the Canteen

The back door creaked. Jessie glanced at the clock on the dresser: there were never any visitors on a Sunday evening. The manageress had left for the sergeant's mess around eight o'clock and wouldn't be back until ten or even later, depending on the number of games of housey-housey. Jessie stopped writing the laundry list and walked towards the scullery to investigate: it was only Miss Taylor, accompanied by Sergeant Brown, but on this occasion they didn't remain in the kitchen. The sergeant wished Jessie 'Good evening', and followed the manageress into the office.

Business was brisk in the bar, so Jessie didn't give any further thought to the matter until she ran out of change. As she approached the half-open door of the office, the sergeant's words made her prick up her ears. 'You can't go on like this, Molly, you must stay in bed and see the doctor.'

The conversation ceased when Jessie tapped on the door. She apologised for the intrusion and quickly changed the pound note for silver. Even if she hadn't heard the remark, a glimpse of Miss Taylor's pallid face was enough to tell her that she was unwell.

Instead of the usual supper party, Sergeant Brown carried two cups of cocoa into the office. Eventually, he returned to inform Jessie that Molly must have the doctor tomorrow.

Having completed the usual round of duties, Jessie took the cash box into the office. Miss Taylor asked her if she had locked up; then said she didn't feel like talking and wished her 'Goodnight.'

The following morning, Miss Taylor's face was half hidden by the sheet as Jessie placed a cup of tea on her locker.

'Jessie, it's no use; I'll have to have the doctor. You'll have to look after the shop until he's been. Cyril will be calling at nine, will you tell him?'

'Couldn't I put a notice on the door, "closed because of illness"?'

'No, it's only for this morning. I'm sure you can manage.'

Jessie didn't share her superior's confidence in her ability to cope single-handed. Nevertheless, she set to work to carry out her own duties as quickly as possible.

Sergeant Brown arrived promptly. He was obviously relieved that the manageress had agreed to see a doctor, and said he would make the arrangements. As he went out, he held the door open for the baker.

Jessie tried to remain calm as she checked the cakes and bread, but the butcher and several other customers had arrived.

Eleven o'clock came, at last. She had just bolted the door when a man, carrying a Gladstone bag, appeared outside. The doctor asked her to remain in the room while he examined the patient, but before he had taken off his coat, there was a bang on the back door.

There was no time to check the delivery. Jessie left the coal man to tip the bags in the coal shed while she returned to the bedroom. Her heart sank when the doctor came from behind the screen and said, 'A light diet and plenty of tepid baths. The patient must stay in bed for at least a week. I'll call again on Wednesday.'

The coalman was still standing at the back door. 'Sign here,' he said brusquely.

Having scribbled her signature, Jessie took the bill to the office and immediately retraced her steps to answer a whistle from the laundryman.

After another trip to the office to collect the money, there was just time to undo the parcel and put on a clean overall before she made the drinks.

'Jessie ... Jessie.'

'Yes, coming.'

Jessie put down the tray of cakes and dashed into the bedroom.

'I was thinking. If Sergeant Brown doesn't arrive until four, it will be too late to send a telegram. Could you go to the village between one and two?'

'Yes, but I must get back; the tea bag is still in the jug.'

When all the men in the coffee bar had been served, she returned to make up the fire, and asked, 'What would you like to eat?'

'Another cup of tea and a few dry biscuits. If you have time later on, perhaps you'll make me a cup of Bovril and some dry toast.'

While she was waiting for the kettle to boil, Jessie started to weigh up some of the rations for the cookhouse, but she had to leave the task half finished in order to take the tray to the patient, wipe the tables in the coffee bar, and place all the dishes to soak in soda water.

Dressed ready for the excursion, she hurried back to the office. Miss Taylor gave her half a crown from her purse, saying, 'I don't know whether it's a penny or tuppence a word, but you know Mrs Hadley's address.'

At the post office, she wrote on the form: 'Urgent. Molly ill. Please send help immediately. Jessie'.

It wasn't until she was on the return journey that a

thought struck her: the cash boxes were wide open in the two bars. She arrived hot foot at the canteen to find Stormy shouting abuse as he banged on the door of the grocery.

Blondie was the first to notice her. 'Hullo, what are you doing out?'

'I'm sorry. I had to go to the village to send a telegram. The manageress is ill.'

Stormy joined in the conversation. 'Old biddy ill? What's happening about the rations?'

'They're nearly ready. Just let me take my coat off.'

'Back in a quarter of an hour, miss, will that do?'

The afternoon passed quickly with Jessie torn between preparing the suppers for the coffee bar and answering the shop bell. Sergeant Brown arrived; then went off to collect the prescription, promising to return later.

At five o'clock, she was at last free. Suddenly she remembered that the dishes were still in the sink and there would be a shortage if she didn't wash them up straight away. There was now no time to prepare a light meal.

Later in the evening, Sergeant Brown came to the rescue by toasting the bread at the office fire and acting as waiter. Before he returned to his bunkhouse, he said, 'Molly's anxious about the grocery bar; I'm going to do some weighing up. You are writing down everything you take?'

Jessie answered in the affirmative and went off to pay for the two bars of chocolate she had eaten on the way to the village. This reminded her that her dinner had consisted of tea and biscuits. She made a meat sandwich, to use up the remains of the Sunday joint, and gulped it down while she was transferring the cookery utensils to the scullery.

By half past eleven all the clearing up had been

completed. Jessie took the cash box to the office, where she found Miss Taylor leaning on the back of the chair. Having smoothed the wrinkles out of the under sheet, and helped the manageress to ease herself gently back into bed, Jessie fetched a chamber pot from her bedroom, insisting that she must not attempt to go outside during the night.

On Tuesday, Miss Taylor drank her morning cup of tea and said she didn't feel like cooked breakfast.

At nine o'clock Jessie was back in the grocery, endeavouring to slice the bacon with a long steel knife. The blade grated on the wooden board and set her teeth on edge as she tried to saw through the thick brown skin. It was easier to remove the rind first; then it dawned on her that rind-less bacon would sell at a loss. With aching shoulder, she persevered until the first customer arrived and purchased most of the ragged rashers.

Another customer required a box of matches, and then added as an afterthought, 'Oh and a pound of sugar please.' This jogged her memory: she hadn't made a note of the sugar she had served on the previous day, but the grocery would have to suffer the loss because the recipient hadn't given her name.

Miss Taylor was standing beside the washbasin when Jessie gave her a mid-morning cup of tea. 'How are you getting on?'

'Not very well. I can't make the cream biscuits the correct weight.'

'Try putting half a broken one in the bag first.'

'I've tried, but it doesn't always work.'

'Have you done the cookhouse order yet?'

'No, I'm just going to do it.'

The large slab of margarine weighed just under four

pounds. Yesterday, Stormy had relied on her honesty when he collected the rations; he probably wouldn't notice if she made everything slightly under weight,

Blondie transferred the rations straight from the counter to the barrow while Stormy signed the chit, but it was still possible for the order to be re-weighed in the cookhouse. Jessie waited anxiously for the sounds of activity over the way before she breathed a sigh of relief.

When the coffee bar opened, Paddy came to the counter. 'You look tired, Scottie.'

'I'm not sure if I'm on my head or my heels. Miss Taylor's ill and she's supposed to have a light diet, but I haven't time to see to it.'

Another customer interrupted the brief conversation.

On Wednesday morning, Stormy requested milk and two eggs. When he gave back the half empty jug, it occurred to Jessie that Miss Taylor might fancy a glass of milk, but it was too late now to retrieve it. She was very grateful when the cook soon returned to pass a bowl of soup and a baked egg custard through the window, with instructions to share it with old biddy.

Throughout the morning, Jessie answered every bell expectantly, but there was still no sign of the relief manageress when she locked the door and resumed her duties in the kitchen.

'Scottie, there's a man knocking on the door of the grocery,' called a voice from the main door of the mess. She hurried into the shop, only to find that it was the doctor. 'Will you see yourself in? I can't leave the bar.'

After a few minutes, the doctor came back with the glad tidings that it wasn't necessary for him to call again. 'Just remember to keep the patient in bed on a light diet. Good day.'

The strain was beginning to tell. It was easy for Miss Taylor, tucked up in bed, to say that she was doing fine, just fine, and to hang on a little longer. The obvious solution was to go against her wishes and send another telegram.

Stormy was waiting quietly at the grocery door when Jessie returned from the post office. 'Any word of old biddy coming back to work?'

'No, she has to rest.'

'Have you contacted the Area Manager?'

'No, I haven't got his address. I've just sent another telegram to her sister. She's manageress at Bury. The supervisors often go there.'

Thank goodness it was Wednesday and most of the men would be on the sports field with some of their wives as spectators: there would only be a few customers in the grocery, and the supper trade would also be light.

Sergeant Brown came to make up the books and commented that the staff messing was negligible. Jessie had already decided that giving short weight to her friend in the cookhouse was not only dishonest, but also disloyal. In any case, it shouldn't be necessary to take such extreme measures to balance the books.

When the bar closed, Jessie was thankful that there was only Miss Taylor's bed to make before she retired for the night. As her own bed hadn't been made since Sunday, she kicked off her shoes and lay down for a few minutes, with the intention of straightening the covers before she undressed.

'Jessie... Jessie ... it's time to get up.'

Jessie thought, for a moment, it was afternoon because she was fully dressed. She pulled herself together and opened the bedroom door to find Miss Taylor, in slippers and dressing gown. 'Jessie, I'm sorry to wake you but fatigues has been banging on the door. It's eight o'clock. I've managed to light the fire.'

In the kitchen, the paper and wood had burnt through but the coal hadn't caught alight. The coalman had taken mean advantage of her plight and delivered huge lumps instead of the requested Welsh nuts.

The next two days dragged by; the Naafi appeared to have forgotten them. Miss Taylor solved the problem of daily deliveries by instructing Jessie to sign the notes, 'received but not checked', leaving Sergeant Brown to deal with them in the evenings. He also did all the heavy work of transferring bulky packages to the stock cupboard and replenished the shelves in the grocery bar. Jessie was grateful for his help in weighing the dry ingredients and keeping the accounts, but even more pleased that he was there to keep his friend company.

On Saturday evening, Jock Craig expounded on the inadequacy of the Naafi management as he drank his pint. 'You know what to do, leave the grocery bar closed.'

'But what about the rations for the cookhouse?'

'That would force the issue: Mr Johnson would be down here in double quick time to sort it out.'

He was right, of course, but the state of emergency was now less acute as the grocery bar was always closed on Saturday afternoon and all day Sunday.

On Sunday, Miss Taylor came to the kitchen, fully dressed, and pottered about, peeling the potatoes and helping with other small tasks. When the bar closed, she volunteered to wash up, but she still looked so pale that Jessie didn't have the heart to leave her alone at the sink. After dinner she went to lie down again, and Jessie was glad to escape into the green countryside for a breath of fresh air.

On Monday morning it was back to the trials and tribulations of the grocery bar.

Jessie was relieved when she returned to the kitchen and found that Miss Taylor had put the kettle on. She managed to take a short break while they drank their tea, and was sorry when her superior returned to her room: it was reassuring to know that she was close at hand.

The bell rang and Mr Johnson came through the shop door. 'Now what's all this? I hear Miss Taylor is ill.'

'Yes, sir.'

'Where is she?'

'In the bedroom, sir, but she's up and dressed now.'

'Is it all right if I go through?'

'I'll find out, sir.'

When he came out of the office, the Area Manager explained that a new manageress had been despatched with instructions to do all she could to help and that Miss Taylor would now take sick leave. He was watching the clock as he spoke: presumably he was anxious to avoid Jock Craig.

Overjoyed, Jessie went to the office and received advance information about Miss Taylor's replacement. Miss Nolan had worked in a grocer's shop, but not in a Naafi canteen. Mrs Hadley had been training her to do the books. As she had only to come from Bury, she should be here by three.

The new manageress duly arrived, looking very smart in her navy-blue suit and white satin blouse. Aged about twenty-six and of medium height, she was sturdily built with a well-proportioned figure. Her fresh complexion and the natural wave of her dark hair complemented her attractive features.

Jessie showed her into the office while she prepared a tray of tea.

The next two hours passed so quickly that it all seemed like a dream. Miss Taylor, a trifle upset, kissed Jessie before she departed with Sergeant Brown as escort.

Jessie gave Miss Nolan clean bedding and directed her to the overalls; then left her to her own devices because she was so busy in the bar.

At the end of the evening, Miss Nolan was uncommunicative when she came out of the office, and soon retired with her cup of cocoa.

16

New Management

The new manageress was dressed ready for work when Jessie took in her early morning cup of tea. She enquired about the noise in the kitchen and responded to the explanation about the cockroaches by saying she considered a packet of Woodbines a day to be excessive; a remuneration of one per week was more than adequate.

Throughout the morning, she continued to ask questions about the routine, commenting that it was difficult to absorb all the details at such short notice.

Jessie had begun the preparations for lunch when Miss Nolan said she would take over, so she went off to celebrate by giving the coffee bar a special clean.

Just before twelve, Jessie checked that the rice pudding, she had prepared earlier had not been forgotten, but the skin was still pale.

The news of the arrival of the new manageress had already circulated. Jock Craig enquired if everything had now returned to normal.

'Oh yes. Miss Nolan is cooking the dinner today. I've managed to catch up with some of my own work.'

'What's happened to Miss Taylor?'

'She's gone on sick leave.'

'Yes, but where has she gone?'

'I don't know. Mr Johnson didn't tell me.'

'Did he say how long she'd be away?'

'No, but Miss Taylor said a while ago that she'd booked her holiday for the third week in June.'

'And when are you going on holiday?'

'When I've worked a year, I'll have a week's holiday with pay. Isn't that good, a week's holiday and paid as well?'

Jock sniffed. 'I think there's something burning in your kitchen.'

Jessie thought he was joking, but when she went to fetch a clean tea towel, she found that the iron saucepan of potatoes had boiled dry.

Having closed the bar and stacked the dishes, Jessie laid the table and went in search of Miss Nolan.

'Are you all right?' she enquired, when she found her sitting at the desk in the office.

'Yes, I took my ring off to wash my hands and thought I'd lost it.'

'It can't have gone far. Perhaps we could look for it after dinner.'

'Oh, it's all right, I found it, eventually, on the chest of drawers.'

Miss Nolan accepted the blame when Jessie told her about the potatoes. They suffered in silence as they ate the burnt sausages, which were raw in the centre and the butter beans, tasting like brine. Jessie consoled herself that there was a nice rice pudding to follow, and was puzzled when she found that the surface was streaked with yellow strands.

'I don't know what's happened to the pudding. It was all right when I looked at it just before twelve.'

'You forgot to add an egg, so I did it for you.'

'But we never put an egg in when we use evaporated milk.'

'Rice pudding should always have an egg.'

In the bar, Jessie ate two cakes and drank a cup of

lukewarm tea as she did the washing up. It would be wrong to pass judgement at such an early stage: Miss Nolan had barely had time to find her feet.

Having completed her own duties, Jessie looked into the grocery bar. 'Shall I show you where everything is before I go to my room?'

'That won't be necessary. I often manage my father's shop.'

By the evening Jessie's good humour had returned. Corporal Harris ordered bacon and eggs instead of his usual sausage sandwich, cut in four. Corporal Skinner said, 'That looks delicious, Scottie, same again please.'

In the kitchen, Miss Nolan was standing in front of the range and didn't step aside to allow the frying pan to be transferred to the ring. 'I shall be doing the cooking from now on,' she declared.

If the supper had been for anyone else, Jessie would not have demurred, but Miss Taylor regarded the immaculate Corporal Skinner as one of her best customers and always took great pains to serve him well. 'I'll just cook this one because I know how the corporal likes his eggs fried.'

'I've just told you. I intend to do the cooking.' The diamond ring sparkled on her smooth, white finger as she picked up the frying pan. 'What does he want?'

'Wouldn't you prefer to serve in the bar while I do the cooking?'

'Certainly not! I'm not going in there with all those soldiers. In any case, I've just got engaged and I must be able to cook.'

This statement only added to Jessie's unease. She made one final plea. 'Please let me do this one. Corporal Skinner is very fussy.'

The new manageress remained adamant. With reluctance, Jessie passed on the order and returned to the bar.

Corporal Skinner looked across in surprise when she served the next two customers with Bass and boot polish. 'You haven't forgotten my supper Scottie?'

'No, it's on the way.'

Back in the kitchen, Jessie took one look at the plate and gasped, 'I can't give that to Corporal Skinner!'

'Why not?'

'He's very fussy and Miss Taylor always takes great care not to upset him.'

'We are not here to cater for fussy people. Give it to him before it goes cold.'

As Jessie carried the plate into the bar, Corporal Skinner jumped to his feet saying, 'Good,' and came to the counter. The astonishment on his face caused Jessie to lapse into hysterical laughter. The eggs, fried on both sides in very hot fat, were brown and speckled; the bacon was shrivelled and the tomatoes were splattered across the plate.

'If this is supposed to be a joke, Scottie, I don't find it the least bit amusing.'

Jessie quickly recovered her composure and explained that the new manageress had taken over the cooking. With a bad grace, the corporal sat down at a table and moodily prodded the solid yolk with his fork. Jessie offered a refund, but he left the one and tuppence on the counter beside the uneaten supper.

Jock walked across to inspect the repast. 'What happened there?'

'The new manageress won't let me do the cooking.'

'If that's the best she can do, wouldn't it be better if you cooked the suppers and she served in the bar?'

'That's the trouble: she won't allow me to do the cooking and she won't serve in the bar because she doesn't like soldiers.'

At that moment there was a scream, followed by a crash. Jessie rushed out to the scullery.

Miss Nolan was standing by the light-switch; the dish that had held the tomatoes lay upturned on the floor. 'The place is running alive. There's hundreds of them. Where's the Keating's powder?'

'We haven't any. It's not worth bothering though. They'll fall in the sink tonight and fatigues will kill them off tomorrow.'

She returned to the bar and met Jock Craig coming through the counter. 'Is she badly hurt?'

He looked surprised when Jessie shrugged, 'No, she just got a fright with the cockroaches.'

The following morning, Miss Nolan was more amenable when she put in an early appearance in the kitchen. Having inspected the cockroaches, she fetched five packets of Woodbines and placed them in the drawer of the dresser, instructing Jessie to give only one packet per day to fatigues. Then she enquired about the usual arrangements for the general assistant's half-day. Jessie explained that she was supposed to be free after dinner, but it depended on how long it took to prepare the suppers. Miss Nolan said there was no need to bother about the catering as she wouldn't be opening the coffee bar.

'Oh, but you must!'

'There is no must about it. I came here as a grocery bar manageress, not a coffee bar assistant.'

'But you can't close the bar without notice.'

'It's no concern of yours. I'm quite capable of making my own decisions, thank you.'

At dinner time, Jessie tried in vain to swallow the semi-cooked meal. When Miss Nolan went to fetch a packet of tea from the grocery, she quickly scraped her plate into the pig bin in the scullery, to avoid giving offence.

After dinner, there were no suppers to prepare, so Jessie took the opportunity to give the neglected kitchen floor a good scrub. It was four o'clock by the time she lay on her bed to recover from the exertion, and make plans for the rest of the day.

If she went to the cinema the first house would be over by eight-thirty and she would be back by nine, unless she whiled away the time in Southport. On the other hand, if she went to the second house, the feature film wouldn't finish until ten-thirty, which meant she would be returning along the lonely road at eleven o'clock. The bar had been open every day since her arrival, six months ago; it was even open on public holidays and during stock-taking. She couldn't help surmising about the reaction of Jock Craig when the work-to-rule deprived him of his pint: no doubt the Area Manager would be summoned, post-haste, to deal with the mutiny.

Jessie awoke with a start and jumped up. She thought she had overslept, but the hands on the clock said five-thirty and it was broad daylight. She sat on the side of the bed and listened to the thumping on the shutters in the coffee bar as it gradually rose to a crescendo. After a short silence, the banging became intermittent. She waited, expectantly, but there was no sound of activity in the kitchen. Finally, the tapping became more rhythmic. She was amused when she recognised the Morse code. It was no use, she couldn't ignore the distress signal S.O.S.

Having exchanged her frock for an overall, Jessie went into the bar. The round of applause, as she started to take down the shutters, ended abruptly as she appeared.

'Where's the manageress?'

'It's your half-day, isn't it, Scottie?'

'I don't know where Miss Nolan is, and it is my half-day, so I haven't made the tea.'

'We've been playing cricket, Scottie. Would you oblige us with some shandies please?'

Jessie served the drinks and, assuming that Miss Nolan had gone out, went into the kitchen to put the kettle on. The meat was still on the marble slab in the larder. In warm weather it was imperative that it was cooked on the day it was delivered. She had just started to make a liver casserole when, to her surprise, Miss Nolan came out of the office. 'What do you think you are doing? This is your half-day. My orders are to see you get it.'

By now, Jessie's patience was exhausted; she answered in the same tone, 'And did you also have instructions to close the coffee bar without notice?'

The manageress was too taken aback to reply, so she continued. 'After the men have had their tea, they always spend the evenings in the mess. There's nowhere open in the village, apart from the pub. The men on duty couldn't get there and back anyway. I've opened the bar tonight, but if you think you know better, I'll send a telegram to Mr Johnson tomorrow, and that will settle the matter.'

Jessie hadn't the faintest idea where Mr Johnson might be found, but her outburst had the desired effect: Miss Nolan retreated to the office and returned with her overall.

During the days that followed the manageress didn't allude to the incident. However, her insistence on cooking the dinner caused Jessie to be out of pocket: she had to pay for the cakes and bars of chocolate she consumed as she did the washing up in the bar. Needless to say, she sighed with relief when the manageress departed at one-thirty on Saturday, without mentioning where she intended to spend her half-day.

Stormy invited Jessie to afternoon tea for the sole purpose of finding out how much overtime she had received for working the extra hours during Miss Taylor's illness. She doubted if she would be entitled to anything extra because the manageress hadn't left the canteen until her replacement arrived. Presumably, she would receive her full pay and sickness benefit.

By eleven o'clock, Jessie was ready to retire for the night, but the manageress hadn't returned. The seconds ticked slowly by as she sat in the kitchen, watching the clock. She locked the outside door and switched on the scullery light. Surely the manageress would have the sense to knock on her bedroom window when she returned.

As she lay in bed, fully dressed, she could hear the sound of laughter in the yard. She switched off the light and peeped through the curtains: it was only a group of sergeants who were chatting before they dispersed at the end of an evening in the mess.

It was well after midnight when she finally decided to undress, and fell asleep almost immediately.

The alarm rang. Jessie washed and dressed quickly. She tapped on the office door and waited. When she peeped in, sunlight was streaming through the open curtains and the screen was still in the daytime position round the bed.

In the kitchen, Jessie tried to concentrate on the chores, but her attention kept wandering back to the hands on the clock. She had just decided to ask Stormy's advice when the back door opened. Miss Nolan walked briskly into the kitchen, saying she had missed the train, and went straight into the office to take off her outdoor clothes.

Jessie was so pleased to see her that she put the tin kettle on and laid a tray. The manageress sat down wearily at the kitchen table and took two aspirins with her cup of tea. Having graciously accepted Jessie's offer to do the cooking, she retired to her room.

Cooking the dinner, in addition to opening the bar, was a feat accomplished more by good luck than judgement.

Miss Nolan complimented Jessie on the roast beef and Yorkshire pudding but, otherwise, said very little during the meal.

'Are you staying in the Naafi after you are married?' The question was really designed to break the silence: Jessie was not particularly interested in what the manageress intended to do after her temporary stay.

'No, I didn't realise the living conditions would be so bad. My father didn't believe me when I told him I'd come home to have a bath.'

'But you could have a shower in the sergeant's mess.'

'I find that arrangement most unsatisfactory.'

'There was a bathroom at Bury and there'll probably be one at your next canteen.'

'I'm not sure there's going to be a next canteen. If I'd known that I'd have to cope with all this, I wouldn't have taken the post.'

'Mr Johnson probably meant you to do the cooking just on my half-day.'

'No, he definitely said I had to do the cooking.'

'I don't mind doing it.'

'No, it's quite all right. After all, practice makes perfect.'

The sun now rose early in the morning and shone throughout the day in a clear, blue sky. Jessie was determined to take advantage of the warm weather and increased hours of daylight: a trip to Southport would make a change from the rigours of the last three weeks. She congratulated herself that, once again, the canteen was spick and span, which only left one problem: she had no idea if the manageress intended to open the coffee bar on her half-day.

Miss Nolan was still persevering with the cooking. As Jessie watched her struggling with the fish slice, she realised that her superior was incapable of minding the bar and cooking the suppers.

On Tuesday morning Jessie tentatively suggested that it was about time they had some more potato pies. There was no point in slaving over a hot stove in this weather. She omitted to mention that Miss Taylor had only ordered them on one occasion because there wasn't enough profit to make them a good proposition.

Miss Nolan added a dozen pies to the baker's order. It seemed to have escaped her notice that they would arrive on Jessie's half-day.

On Wednesday morning the manageress was quite amiable when she came into the kitchen and lingered by the stove. Then she went into the coffee bar, for no apparent reason, and Jessie wondered if she was familiarising herself with the layout: she had not set foot in there since her arrival. The indications were that she had changed her mind about opening the bar, but Jessie didn't mention her half-day and neither did she.

After dinner, Jessie went to the bedroom to change, and looked out of the window at the cloudless sky. The soldiers would be enjoying the cricket match and would return suntanned, cheerful and very thirsty. If Miss Nolan didn't intend to remain in the service, a reprimand from the Area Manager wouldn't bother her. It would be very hot on the beach at Southport, and then there was the problem of what to do during the long, lonely evening. It was senseless to allow her own obstinacy to prevent her from enjoying the highlight of an otherwise dreary existence.

Miss Nolan was obviously surprised when she found Jessie stoking the stove at four o'clock, but she made no comment and enquired what she would like for supper.

'Something cool – like tinned pears.'

The manageress began to lay the table, and Jessie started to prepare for the opening.

156

Miss Nolan asked, 'Are we just going to sell sandwiches?'

'I thought we'd put the potato pies on the menu.'

'Oh yes, I'd forgotten about them.'

After the evening meal, the manageress actually started to wash up, which gave Jessie plenty of time to remove the shutters before the men arrived.

Jock Craig was first at the counter, as usual. 'I thought this was your day off.'

'I'm going to ask for extra time off when Miss Taylor comes back.'

'When is the Area Manager due to call?'

'I don't know.'

'No, I expect he's making himself scarce. If he does show his face, tell him I'd like to see him.'

Some of the cricket team arrived, but it was not until they had been served with shandies that they remembered it was Jessie's half-day.

'Is the manageress still refusing to serve us?'

'Well, I was a bit shy myself when I came...'

'Shy, come off it, Scottie! If she can serve us in the grocery, there's no reason why she can't serve us in here.'

On Thursday morning, Miss Nolan passed a postcard across the breakfast table. The message was that Miss Taylor was much better and would be going on holiday the following week. Jessie's relationship with Miss Nolan had now improved, but her spirits rose as she read the final words: back on Saturday 22nd.

The days passed quickly and Wednesday came round once again. At five-thirty, Miss Nolan started to prepare for the increased demand for cold items such as corned beef and pickles.

Jessie was serving the customers, and enjoying the atmosphere of the crowded bar, when Paddy and Stan arrived together. Paddy enquired, 'Are those pies on the board real or imaginary?'

'Oh they're real, I ordered them especially for Private Eccles.'

'That's all right,' said Paddy, 'as long as there's Irish stew on the menu tomorrow.' He carried the two plates to join Stan at a table; then stacked the cups and saucers left by previous customers, before he sat down. When he had finished his pie, he returned the tray of crockery and leaned on the counter. 'When is Molly coming back?'

'She's on holiday next week. I think she's going to Scarborough.'

'Sure now, I miss her haughty ways.' He tossed his head in perfect mimicry. 'Private Riley, how long is it going to take you to drink all those cups of tae? Miss Edmondstone has work to do. She can't stand there all day, keeping you company.'

One of the men at the billiards table looked across and called, 'What's Paddy got that I haven't got?'

'Nothing, apart from a tray of dirty pots,' he replied quickly; then requested two cups of tea.

Later in the evening, it was so hot in the bar that Jessie's hair felt wet on the back of her neck. As soon as there was a lull, she went to her bedroom to fix her plaits.

On her return, she could hear Jock Craig saying, 'It's a sewing kit – the bottom drawer on the right.'

'Do you know how much it costs?' There was no mistaking the clear pronunciation of the female voice in the bar.

'I'm not sure,' said Jock Craig.

Before Jessie had time to grasp what was happening, Nobby held up the linen pack, containing needles and thread, and called out. 'Anyone know the worth of a housewife?'

'More precious than rubies,' called a voice from the back of the mess.

'But only if she can cook,' commented another.

The manageress blushed to the roots of her hair. Jessie couldn't help feeling sorry for her as she attempted to make a dignified exit.

Miss Nolan's departure left Jessie with mixed feelings. She now realised that they had one thing in common: their perfunctory training had not prepared either of them for their particular role in the institutes.

17

Taking Risks

On her return, the re-invigorated Miss Taylor resumed her usual lifestyle. Jessie observed that, in one respect, the manageress was just like Miss Nolan: she liked to know all the news, but didn't disclose a single detail about her convalescence or vacation.

Miss Taylor found Jessie's account of the events of the past three weeks very amusing. The thought of the disgusted Corporal Skinner was particularly hilarious, probably because Jessie had related the tale so mournfully, expecting her to be upset at the loss of her best customer.

Having enquired about Sergeant Brown, and that old curmudgeon in the cookhouse, the manageress returned to the subject of the boyfriend, whom Jessie had not yet managed to acquire. Apart from Jock Craig, the only other person who chatted with Jessie was Paddy Riley – and just recently he hadn't been his usual cheerful self.

Everything was now back to normal in the canteen, except that the heat wave had resulted in an increased demand for cold drinks and fewer requests for snacks. Nevertheless, the range had still to be stoked at frequent intervals, and even when the casement windows were wide open, the temperature was at times unbearable. The coffee bar was also stuffy because cigarette smoke stagnated in the alcove, making the atmosphere even more intolerable than the heat of the kitchen.

161

One evening, Jessie was washing the glasses with beads of perspiration trickling down her nose, when it occurred to her that if she opened the hatch, there would be a through draught. She lifted aside the crates to open the small door and was startled by a voice. 'Good evening, Scottie.'

'Oh, it's you Private Pompey. Are you all by yourself?

'Yes, it's much cooler in here.' The Private stood up and ran his hand over his straight, black hair to lift a strand off his high forehead. 'You look terribly hot, Scottie.'

'Yes, that's why I opened the hatch.'

'Do you have to wear that hat?'

'It's one of the regulations.'

His grey eyes twinkled. 'Oh, I forgot. The Naafi wouldn't allow you to take off one of your labels. You might be purloined!'

This remark made Jessie giggle. Almost everything in the canteen had the Naafi crest painted, stamped or embroidered on it; the badge was even carved on the round backs of the wooden armchairs in the bar.

'Did you want a drink?'

'A shandy please – and have one yourself.'

'Oh no, thank you, I don't drink.'

'Well, a lemonade then.'

'It's very nice of you but I'm not allowed to.'

Jessie poured the shandy, then there was no more time to chat because the rest of the customers were all very thirsty.'

Miss Taylor kept ahead with her work because she was determined to enjoy the fine weekends. Jessie was left to her own devices, except that she now had to learn the books, an irksome task, but one which was obviously in her best interests.

Sergeant Brown still came to supper, but at the weekend he was often playing tennis or cricket. Jessie could understand why Miss Taylor was so taken with him: he looked so distinguished in his white flannels and navy blue blazer with a badge on the breast pocket. It seemed a pity that they should just remain good friends: he was firm but gentle and extremely tolerant of her erratic temperament. However, Jessie had neither the time nor the inclination to pry into the affairs of anyone else, she was always too absorbed with her own. Her savings were now sufficient to pay for a whole new outfit. When Miss Taylor told her to stop dithering, she made up her mind to go to Ormskirk on a shopping expedition.

It was the first time Jessie had bought any clothes for herself, and when the shop assistant assured her that the brown worsted coat was a good fit, she parted with fifty-nine shillings. Miss Taylor wasn't very enthusiastic about her purchase: the coat hung like a sack on her slim figure. Jessie not only regretted her extravagance, but also the loss of the sense of security that her savings had given her.

It was now the third week in July and Jessie suddenly sensed that there was something wrong at home. Mam was constantly in her thoughts, especially when she was alone in the kitchen. Miss Taylor noticed she was not as cheerful as usual when Sergeant Brown entertained them with his impersonation of Leslie Sarony, singing, 'I lift up my finger and say tweet, tweet, shoo, shoo, now, now, come, come.' Normally, she would have been interested in the latest show at the Pier Pavilion, but she was in no mood for frivolity and found his song ridiculous rather than amusing.

When the sergeant returned to his bunkhouse, Miss

Taylor mentioned that there was an excursion from Southport to Carlisle on the following Sunday, and asked Jessie if she would like to go, in lieu of the half days she had missed.

It wasn't until she was sitting on the train, surrounded by trippers, that Jessie remembered Charles was coming that day; therefore the arrangement was mutually convenient.

Mam came into the scullery as soon as she heard the door being opened. ' Oh, it's you Jessie!'

In the living room, Mary and Jamie were sitting in the armchairs, listlessly staring at the pictures in comics. Jessie was shocked to see how emaciated they had become. 'What caused them to get so thin?'

'You may well ask,' said Mam wearily. 'They've both had whooping cough. They get into a spasm of coughing, and just when I'm sure they're going to choke, they vomit. They just can't keep food down.'

As the conversation continued, it became apparent that shortage of money was also contributing to her anxiety. Every time the doctor called, the fee was a shilling, and then there were all the delicacies she had prepared to tempt the invalids. She couldn't help comparing Jessie with her sister: although Anna paid her board, she couldn't be persuaded to part with any of her bonus.

There were tears in Mam's eyes as she held out the photograph of the school swimming team, with John on the front row. She had intended to take an excursion to London, but now all her savings had been spent. Her distress caused Jessie to regret her recent extravagance: she could only give her mother the pound in her purse.

After a snack lunch, Jessie spent the afternoon amusing the children, but the time passed all too quickly. It was not long before she was once again on the train, lost in thought.

Mam couldn't understand Anna's attitude that 'if yir kind, people just think yir daft' because she, herself, had a kindly nature. Anna was more like father: she had not only inherited his auburn hair, she had also been outspoken and uncompromising since an early age.

Although John was only two years older than Anna, he was much more mature. Jessie had missed her constant companion when he went to Dunblane. Father had decided his son must receive a good education; Mam had argued that a nine-year-old lad, with a quiet disposition, would find it difficult to fend for himself. Father had accused her of being over protective and had made all the arrangements, despite her protests.

John had lived up to his father's academic expectations and had also excelled at sport, but he looked forward to the holidays when he would spend many happy hours, sitting on the riverbank, waiting silently for a fish to rise to the bait. He didn't want to enlist for a career in the army, and Mam had promised him faithfully that, as soon as he was old enough, he could leave school and find a job.

When John was due to come home on his final school holiday, Mam sent a postal order to pay his fare, but the letter was returned with his new address at Wellington Barracks in London. In high dudgeon, she wrote to the Adjutant to complain that she hadn't given permission for her son to join the Scots Guards. The curt reply was that his father was named as guardian when John was admitted to the school therefore he had the authority to sign the papers. The arrangements had presumably been made when Father took William to enrol. John was obviously resentful that he had been enlisted against his will, and also very hurt that Mam had, apparently, broken her promise.

*　*　*

At Southport, Jessie stopped a porter to enquire the time of the next train.

'Sorry miss, the last train's gone. I'm just going to close the station.' He walked along the platform and started to usher a group of stranded passengers through the exit.

Jessie checked the contents of her purse: the return half of the ticket and one shilling. The porter was still arguing with a group of people at the exit, so she walked down the ramp.

It was unusual for people to walk along the track in England whereas, in Scotland, it was quite a common occurrence. The depression had caused mass unemployment. When men were subjected to a means test, the wages of their sons and daughters were assessed as the income of the household. Rather than be supported by their families, they went on tramp through the towns and villages in search of casual labour. Down on their uppers, they often abandoned the rough roads to walk on the sleepers.

Jessie hadn't gone far when the railway lines started to converge and disappeared into the darkness ahead. A shout from somewhere above startled her. She looked up and could see a man, leaning out of the window of a signal box. He called to her to stand quite still and stay where she was; it dawned on her that, even if there were no more passenger trains, a goods train could be on the way through.

The signalman climbed down the side of the box and again called, 'Stay where you are. Don't move.' Slowly and carefully he picked his way across the tracks. When he reached her, he said quietly, 'Just follow me and don't touch the rails.'

Each time he crossed a line, he turned to watch her progress. 'Be careful of this one,' he said as he stepped carefully over a rail, and then stood still while she negotiated it.

166

When they reached a sidewalk between some houses, he suddenly flared up. 'Don't you know those rails carry thousands of volts?' He lifted his elbow as if to strike her. 'Clear off, before I report you for trespass.'

Jessie hurried away, trying to decide which way to go. She had never heard of volts, and as she had paid for her ticket, she thought his hostility was completely unjustified.

The sound of footsteps behind her caused her to panic. She took to her heels and ran until the blue lamp of a police station came in sight. At the door, she stopped to regain her breath, but her heart was still pounding as she told the policeman she had missed her train. He called another constable. 'This young woman has been stranded. Take her along to the bakery and see if one of the delivery vans will give her a lift.'

As they walked along the street, Jessie explained that the excursion train must have been delayed because she was too late to catch a connection. Close to tears, she told him the manageress would be very angry because she was supposed to be back by eleven.

At the bakery, the constable went inside and returned with the news that nothing would be going out before five. However, he said he would lend her the money for a taxi, and they set out to find one. Eventually, they came across a car, with the engine running, but the driver had had a long day and was reluctant to take a late night fare. Eventually he agreed, partly as a favour, but also for payment in advance. The policeman then wrote in his notebook and tore out the page. 'That's seven and sixpence you owe me. Make sure you pay it back.'

Jessie's first journey in a motorcar was nerve-racking. The headlights beamed on the road ahead, but she couldn't identify the black objects flashing past the windows. Eventually, the cab slowed down and swung round outside the entrance to the Depot.

'Half a minute,' said the driver, but she had gone, leaving the door swinging on its hinge.

Having wrestled with the bolted yard door, she tapped frantically on the office window. Miss Taylor's head appeared, decked in curling pins.

'Could I borrow seven and six to pay a policeman?'

'Of course, where is he?'

'At Southport.'

'Well you can't pay him tonight if he's at Southport!'

In the kitchen, the manageress listened to the garbled account and then burnt some firewood to boil the kettle. Jessie was grateful that she was so sympathetic, especially when she promised to allow her time off in the morning to go to the post office.

After the postal order had been despatched, Jessie tried to forget the nightmare, but in the evening, Paddy Riley's first words were, 'Did the search party find you last night, Scottie?'

'Search party?'

'Molly and the Sarge were at the station last night. They asked me if I'd seen you at Southport.'

'Oh, I missed my connection and came back by taxi.'

'Doing things in style, eh?'

Corporal Graves struck up 'Life on the Ocean Wave'. Jessie was grateful for the diversion and took the opportunity to go out and collect the glasses. When she was near the door, the pianist launched into a selection of Scottish reels.

'You're supposed to dance a jig to that, Scottie,' said one of the soldiers.

'Like this?' She crossed a knife and fork on the floor; raised her arms and danced a few steps. She hadn't anticipated that her brief display would attract so much attention, and glanced round in surprise at the polite applause. At that moment, she noticed the expression on Pompey's face as he looked anxiously across the bar in the direction of Jock Craig, who had straightened himself up to his full height and was flapping one hand up and down on his posterior. Jessie quickly picked up the cutlery and carried the tray to the counter.

Paddy had been perched on the edge of one of the tables, but when he saw what was happening, he was quickly on his feet. Holding himself erect, with his hands by his side, he step-danced lightly across the floor.

Miss Taylor's arrival had been obscured by Jock Craig's large frame. She looked round suspiciously: clapping usually meant that someone was waiting for service. The music ended and there was another round of applause as Paddy walked across to the counter to collect a cup of tea.

The comment of the manageress was scathing. 'I might have known it was you, Private Riley. Don't you yet know the difference between a Scottish reel and an Irish jig?'

'No ma'am,' he replied. 'Am I not a poor ignorant spalpeen of a bhoy?'

'You said it,' she said disdainfully, and marched into the kitchen.

Stan and Tug had arrived, just in time to see the end of Paddy's dance routine.

'We didn't know you could dance like that,' said Tug.

'Sure now, everyone dances in the owld country.'

'How about an encore?'

'No, no,' replied Paddy.

When they tried to persuade him, Jessie was surprised that he was so bashful.

'I was only the decoy, you missed the best part.'

'What was that?'

'The Scottish rear-guard action,' he replied with a nod towards Jock Craig.

The pun was wasted on the two latecomers: he didn't bother to enlighten them.

Jessie was pleased that he had now regained some of his former exuberance.

18

Not Quite Cricket

It had taken Jessie eight months but, at last, she had found an inexpensive leisure activity. After an initial outlay of two and eleven pence for a red bathing costume, she looked forward with eager anticipation to each half-day, when she would escape from the heat of the kitchen to slide down the chute into the cool, refreshing water of the open air pool at Southport. She could then while away the hours on the sea front, or in the shopping centre, and return to the canteen at sundown, glowing with contentment.

Miss Taylor gave a hand with the preparation of the suppers, and even suggested that she should casually mention she was going swimming: one of the men would be sure to offer to accompany her.

'Oh, I couldn't do that. They'd see me with no clothes on.'

'Well, fancy that now, and I always thought you went into the water fully dressed! What about Private Belcher?'

'Private Belcher?'

'Yes, Cyril says he's a nice fellow.'

'I don't know who he is.'

The manageress eyed her quizzically. 'Oh really, Cyril seems to think he's quite sweet on you.'

'If you see him in the mess, would you point him out?'

'Yes, but come to think of it, he's probably one of the cricket team.'

'I'd like to know who he is, but I'm not bothered, really, I'm used to being on my own.'

'You surely don't intend to work for the Naafi for the rest of your life.'

'No, I'd like to get married one day.'

'If you don't find someone soon, you'll end up on the shelf. The only way to get a home of your own is to get married.'

'It's manners to wait until I'm asked.'

'They won't ask unless you give them some encouragement.'

'My mother says it's man's place to try and woman's to deny.'

Miss Taylor started to laugh, so Jessie added quickly, 'In any case, I'd rather pay my own way.'

'You're not in Aberdeen now. In England, a gentleman is quite prepared to pay for a lady's company.'

'I don't want to be under an obligation to anyone.'

'If you must be so independent, why don't you go Dutch?'

'What do you mean?'

'You both pay your own expenses.'

The shop bell put an end to the discussion, but Jessie decided to adopt the Dutch system, which must be an accepted alternative to the English rules of convention or Miss Taylor wouldn't have made the suggestion.

Jessie had now come to the conclusion that her superior was a spinster not by choice, but because she had let slip the opportunity to tie the knot.

Sergeant Brown was now reluctant to stay to supper, and had allowed the lessons in accountancy to lapse. Although Jessie had to endure Miss Taylor's sharp rebukes, she couldn't help feeling sorry for her: it was obvious that he was trying to let her down lightly.

Paddy Riley was also frequently lost in thought as he

absentmindedly stirred his tea. Jessie didn't wish to appear inquisitive and made no attempt to find out the reason for his abstraction, until one evening when he was alone at the counter.

Pompey had been in the beer bar since opening time, chatting to Jessie about cricket at every available opportunity. Paddy made no attempt to attract her attention, but waited patiently until she became aware that he was standing at the counter. He was so distant when he requested a cup of tea that she couldn't help enquiring if something was wrong.

'Now what makes you think something is wrong?'

'I don't know, but I'm sure there's something the matter. Is there anything I can do?'

'No, Mavoureen, I made a mistake and now I'll have to pay for it.'

Presuming that he had made a mistake at work, Jessie asked, 'Will it cost very much to put right?'

'That's what you call telepathy, Mavoureen. Wasn't I after thinking that the price was rather high?'

It was obvious that he didn't wish to discuss the matter, so she returned to the hatch, where Pompey was waiting to acquaint her with the rules of cricket.

'Are you in the cricket team, Private Pompey?'

'Yes, but I do wish you would call me Bill.'

'Miss Taylor says there must be no familiarity with the troops. I'd rather call you Private Pompey.'

'If you must be so formal, at least call me by my correct name.'

'But your name's Pompey, isn't it?'

'No, it's a nickname, Belcher is my surname.'

'Then why does everyone call you Pompey?'

'In the army, the Whites are all Chalky; the Wilsons are all Tug; the Clarks are all Nobby; the Scots are all Jock and the Welsh are all Taffy.'

173

'Oh I see.' She really was none the wiser: he hadn't disclosed his own connection with the ancient city, buried under a volcano.

At this point in the conversation, she glanced across at the counter: there were no prospective customers and Paddy was still drinking his tea. He looked so dejected that she started to walk towards him, with the intention of asking him his real name, but as she approached, he finished his tea and said, formally, 'Goodnight, Scottie.'

He walked briskly towards the door; Jessie waited for his usual saucy wink, but this time he didn't look back.

During the winter months Jessie had taken an enlightened interest in the heated arguments about football, but she was completely baffled by the vocabulary of the English game of cricket. When Pompey explained the rules, it was difficult to concentrate with one eye on the counter, so she just tried to appear intelligent while he chatted enthusiastically about short legs, ducks, and bowling a maiden over.

At lunchtime on a hot Saturday afternoon in August, Corporal Harris came to the counter with an unusual request. 'Scottie, could you possibly help us out? We've washed our shirts for the cricket match, but all the heating has been turned off and we can't iron them. Is there any chance...?'

'I'll do my best. Where are they?'

He fetched a large brown paper parcel and placed it on the counter.

'We must have them by two, Scottie.'

Jessie's heart sank: it was now almost one o'clock. 'Do you mean the match is at half past two?'

'No, three o'clock, but we need time to change before we make our way to the field.'

'All right, I'll be as quick as I can.'

'Thanks, Scottie,' he said, with obvious relief. 'One of the men will be waiting here to receive them.'

Jessie hurried to the kitchen to put the flat irons on the range and then put up the shutters. The bar was littered with trays of dirty crockery but there was no time to lose. She quickly cleared the kitchen table in order to spread out the blanket and ironing sheet.

Miss Taylor came into the kitchen, dressed in a tailored cotton dress. 'And pray, what might you be doing?'

Jessie explained about the cricket team's predicament.

'Hmm, on a hot day like this, you really are silly. Florrie was always washing things for them. Don't you start that!'

'No, I won't.'

Miss Taylor's tone indicated that she wasn't in a good humour, despite the fact that she was going out, but Jessie was too busy struggling with the shirts to ponder upon the cause of her testiness. The bone-dry cotton fabric would scorch if the iron were too hot, so the temperature had to be regulated by frequent tests on tissue paper. As there wasn't time to damp the shirts down, she pressed out the creases with a wet tea towel, then ironed the fabric dry.

At two twenty-five, she wiped the perspiration from her face with the wet tea towel, and carried the parcel into the bar. When she shot back the bolt and opened the door under the shuttered counter, it was Paddy Riley who was sitting on the other side. He knelt down and said, 'You did them, Scottie?'

'Yes, Paddy, I made it. I did all the tops but I didna' have time to do the t–.' She pulled herself up sharply: modesty prohibited her from mentioning the tail of a man's shirt. Paddy leaned forward to press his cool lips on her hot cheek. 'You really are a very nice girl, Scottie.'

The compliment was delivered with such sincerity that,

for a moment, she remained on all fours with her head under the counter, but when she stood up, the chaos in the bar brought her back to reality.

The entire afternoon was then taken up with the chores. There was only just enough time to wash and plait her hair before the bar was due to re-open.

For the first time ever, the mess was deserted. Even Jock Craig wasn't in his usual place beside the counter. Jessie returned to the kitchen to prop open the back door with one of the flat irons, and entice Tibby into the yard with a saucer of milk. The Depot was strangely silent and the heat was stifling. She fetched a newspaper and used it as a fan while she sat beside the kitchen window, awaiting the arrival of the customers. It was unusual that there was no one in the cookhouse at teatime. Supposing they had all gone to the pub? She couldn't write off all the suppers!

The din from the direction of the bar suddenly broke the silence.

'We won!' called Corporal Harris triumphantly, as Jessie came into the bar.

The men were jubilant and drank half-pint shandies to celebrate. There had never been such a hubbub in the mess. Everyone seemed to be talking at once as they discussed the finer points of the match.

'What are you having, Scottie, a Bass or a Guinness?'

'No thank you, I don't drink.'

'We'll treat you to a box of chocolates.'

Jessie laughed as they tried to purchase the display dummy.

Two rounds of shandies were quickly followed by a round of suppers. Jessie was surprised they were all so hungry on a warm evening, until she remembered they had missed their tea.

At nine twenty-five she called, 'Any more drinks before I close?'

'Oh Scottie, you can't close yet, we're going to have a session.'

'I must close at half past nine. I'm not allowed to open later without permission.'

'Well then, let's have a few crates out here.'

She hesitated.

'How about it, Scottie? We'll look after the glasses and bottles. We promise to pay if we break any.'

As Miss Taylor hadn't returned, she reluctantly agreed to their request. Two of the men came behind the counter and lifted out the crates, but it was nine forty-five before they had settled up.

With a sigh of relief, Jessie put up the last shutter and wearily set to work on the stack of dishes in the bar, followed by the pile on the kitchen table. She had just finished when Miss Taylor flounced into the kitchen on her own.

'Would you mind if I go to bed?' Jessie's question was more by way of an apology than a request.

'No one's stopping you!' The manageress was in a bad mood, but Jessie was too tired to care, and fell asleep as soon as her head touched the pillow.

Early rising had become part of Jessie's routine. On Sunday morning she was awake at the usual time, despite the fact that she hadn't wound the alarm clock.

In the kitchen, the coal was reluctant to catch alight and there was no mug of tea from Stormy. Eventually, the fire kindled, but the kettle was slow to boil and there was only just time to take Miss Taylor a cup of tea before she hurried off to church.

Since her illness, the manageress had been cooking the breakfast but, on Jessie's return, she was sitting at the table, smoking. She said she didn't want breakfast, just a slice of toast. When Jessie mentioned she had hidden the pound notes in the drawer of the desk because the takings were higher than usual, she made no comment and puffed on her third cigarette. Having drunk her tea, she went into the office, leaving the half-eaten toast on her plate.

At ten-thirty, Jessie was surprised when Miss Taylor tersely reminded her to put the joint in the oven and do the vegetables. She would have done this automatically as part of the Sunday morning routine. Perhaps Miss Taylor was annoyed about the shirts but, so far, she hadn't mentioned the rust-stained tea towel.

The men came over to the coffee bar, after their dinner in the cookhouse, and there was a run on cups of tea. Jock Craig was the only person to request a pint of bitter.

Jessie was apologetic. 'Would you mind having a Whitbreads, corporal? I sold out of bitter last night.'

'That will be all right,' he replied.

'How many times do I have to tell you not to let the beer run out?'

The angry rebuke startled Jessie.

'I won't tell you again,' said the manageress haughtily, and stalked into the kitchen.

Jessie was acutely conscious of the hush in the mess. After a pause, it was Tug who broke the silence. 'She's just come back from Mass, hasn't she? That's what you call a Catholic!'

'I'm a Catholic as well, Tug.' Jessie spoke up quickly to prevent any further comments.

'I'm sorry, Scottie, I wouldn't have said that if I'd known you were a Catholic!'

Mortified by Tug's remark, Jessie swallowed hard to prevent the tears from overflowing. There were customers waiting to be served, but she couldn't face them, and hid in the alcove to splash cold water on her eyes.

'We want you, Scottie.'

'Scottie, come here a minute… Please come here a minute.'

Jessie ignored Pompey's persuasive voice. Miss Taylor would hear them and when she came to see what was happening, she could serve them.

'Scottie, we want to show you something.'

There was a tap on the counter, followed by Jock's gruff voice. 'Come along miss, I want a pint.'

Jessie dried her eyes on a tea towel and turned round to find a crowd at the counter.

'Come here, Scottie. Don's going to show you his book.'

The book, 'not suitable for little girls to see', was placed on the counter.

On the first page there was a pencil sketch of a plump-faced Naafi girl, minus cap and tie, looking very dishevelled. At the top of the page was written: 'We've had this'.

On the next page there was another canteen girl with an enormous cigarette holder; the title was, 'And this'.

Jessie's vision was blurred with tears but, as the pages were turned, she was fascinated by each whimsical sketch, entitled, 'And this'.

The hat of one girl was at a jaunty angle; her tie hung like a noose around the open neck of her overall.

The face of another was partly obscured by a beer glass, raised as a toast.

There was no mistaking Mrs Shane's attractive features and out-going smile.

The final portrait was a girl, with cap set squarely on her head and her hair neatly plaited round her ears. Above the trim figure was the title, 'and at last we have this'. The caption, written underneath, was: 'Servitor Servientium, second to none'.

'It's me. Is it me?'

'Of course it's you. Who else could it be?'

179

'Oh, my mother would like to see it. Please would you lend it to me?'

Private Crosby said, 'I'm sorry, Scottie, I can't spoil the book, but I'll do one for you.'

'Now, miss, can I have a Whitbread?' said Jock Craig, and everything was back to normal in the bar.

It was not so in the kitchen, where the atmosphere was frigid. The silence was unbroken as the manageress shared the meal, which Jessie had cooked. The accusation was not only uncalled for but also untrue: apart from Jessie's first day in the bar, the barrel had never run out.

After dinner, Jessie tidied the kitchen and went to lie down. When she awoke, she lay on the bed and pondered over the events of the last forty-eight hours. Although she was annoyed with Miss Taylor, she was more vexed that she had lost her self-control. If she had remained calm, the incident would soon have been forgotten. The men would have dismissed the remark as just another example of her superior's irascibility. On the other hand, if the soldiers hadn't been filled with indignation, they wouldn't have persuaded Don to reveal the contents of his book.

At first sight, Jessie had presumed the drawings were caricatures, but now she remembered that Don hadn't poked fun at the physical attributes of her predecessors. Vera's voluptuous figure wasn't exaggerated, her pose was characteristic: a cigarette between two oval fingernails as she titivated her hair. Her own portrait was very flattering, offering service with the faintest glimmer of a smile.

Her good humour restored, Jessie had just started to lay the table for tea, when Sergeant Brown came out of the office and requested that she sit down as he wished to have a word with her. He explained that Molly was upset because they had had an argument. He then confided that they had been keeping company for some time, on the understanding that their friendship was purely platonic.

180

Recently, Molly had become more serious and wanted him to break with his fiancé, but this was out of the question: the wedding had already been arranged. He placed two pretty diamante hair slides on the table. 'She sent you these as a peace offering.'

'It was just that I did all the work, even though I'd ironed the shirts – and Paddy Riley was so pleased he kissed me and said I was a very nice girl.'

The sergeant looked alarmed, hesitated for a moment, and then said; 'You do know that Paddy Riley goes to Preston once a month!'

'No.'

'Jessie, this is a very delicate subject and I think you should discuss it with Molly.'

The sergeant said he wouldn't come again, as this would only exacerbate the situation; then shook hands before he left.

When tea was ready, Jessie called Miss Taylor, who had attempted to disguise her red eyes with powder. Having thanked her for the hair slides, Jessie couldn't contain her curiosity any longer. 'Sergeant Brown said that Paddy Riley goes to Preston. He couldn't explain why, and said to ask you.'

The manageress thought for a moment before she answered 'That's because he's having treatment for venereal disease.'

'What's that?'

'It's very infectious.'

'I've never heard of it.'

'I don't suppose you have. No one ever mentions it in public because it's against the law.'

'Against the law?'

'The law of decency.'

The manageress anticipated the next question and tried to demonstrate the effects of the disease. She stood up

181

and swung her legs in such a peculiar fashion that Jessie started to laugh. 'I shan't tell you any more,' she said irritably, and sat down.

'I'm sorry, I won't laugh again, but you looked so funny I thought you were joking.'

'You wouldn't find it quite so funny if your friend Paddy Riley started to walk like that.'

The thought of step-dancing Paddy, reduced to a deformed cripple, made Jessie feel sick inside. 'How do you catch it?'

The manageress puffed at her cigarette. 'Through having intercourse with someone who's got it, but they say you can get it through a cut on your skin, or sometimes through kissing.'

Jessie put her hand to her cheek. 'If someone kissed you on the cheek, would you catch it?'

'I don't know. I expect you would, if you had a cold sore.'

'Has anyone else got it, apart from Paddy Riley?'

'Not that I know of, the men have medical inspections quite frequently. That's why it's better to marry a soldier than a civilian.'

That night Jessie couldn't sleep. She was sure Paddy wouldn't have kissed her if he'd known she'd catch the disease. She tossed and turned, trying to fathom out how it was transmitted. Throughout the winter her hands had been chapped. If the germs could enter through cuts, it was possible that she had already contracted the unmentionable illness through ignorance.

19

For Better for Worse

The heat wave was over, but the legacy of flies flitted around the kitchen until they unsuspectingly alighted on the flypapers and became affixed to the sticky glue. Miss Taylor waged war on the bluebottles, which tantalised her by crawling sleepily on the windowpanes, then darted away as she swiped at them wildly with a newspaper. Apart from the times when she was purging the kitchen of the winged enemy, she was very subdued. Jessie was unable to find amusing snippets to arouse her interest: Paddy Riley hadn't set foot in the bar since the cricket match, and it was quiet on the kitchen front because Stormy was on leave.

There were some new arrivals at the Depot, including a sergeant in his late thirties. He was slightly built, considering that he was five foot six, and not unattractive, despite his lean, sharp features and lank, fair hair. When he first appeared in the mess, he stood beside the door, surveying the scene; then strode over to the counter. 'What have you got to eat, miss?' he asked, eyeing Jessie up and down.

'The menu is on the board.'

'Not much of a selection! Where I come from, one could order a meal that could be classed as a supper.'

Jessie started to pour a second cup of tea for a private.

'You're supposed to be serving me.'

'I'm sorry, I thought the menu was not to your liking.'

'You haven't even taken my order.'

'I haven't time to wait for you to make up your mind.'

Having served the private, Jessie returned to the sergeant. 'Have you decided what you want?'

'Is that all you have?' His voice was patronising as he jerked his thumb in the direction of the board.

'Yes ... apart from bacon and eggs. We can't offer much variety because we don't serve many suppers.'

'If there was more variety, the demand would increase.'

'We haven't the facilities and, in any case, this canteen doesn't pay for itself.'

The sergeant ordered two cheese sandwiches. Before he paid, he poked them with his finger. 'Are these fresh?'

'The bread was delivered this morning. The sandwiches were made at five o'clock, just before I opened the bar.'

He sprawled across the counter. 'You've forgotten my half pint of bitter.'

She pulled the beer very carefully, to ensure it would meet with his approval.

Holding the glass up to the light, he commented, 'It doesn't compare with the beer from my brewery in London.'

Jessie was relieved when the sergeant picked up his supper and walked away, but he selected a table near the counter and sat watching her as she served. After a while, he returned for another half pint. 'Well, when am I taking you out?'

She was annoyed at his audacity and replied, 'I'm sorry, I've already arranged to go out with a friend.'

'I suppose he's a private.' His lips curled in disdain.

'I don't think that is any of your business,' she answered quietly.

'That's as maybe. What did you say your name was?'

'Miss Edmondstone.'

'No, your Christian name.'

'I'm not a Christian,' she said with a smile, because she didn't wish to appear uncivil.

'Oh well, Jock, so be it, you can tell me your name when I take you out next week.'

Jock Craig had only drunk half his beer, so he called Jessie over on the pretext that he needed a stamp. By the time she had fetched one from her room, the sergeant had sat down again. Jock leaned over the counter and said, quietly, 'You don't have to serve him if you don't want to. He's not supposed to come into the men's mess.'

At supper time Jessie was still so incensed by the sergeant's panache that she rashly repeated the conversation word for word. When she said she had arranged to meet a friend, Miss Taylor pricked up her ears. 'And pray, who might that be?'

'Pompey, I mean Private Belcher.' Jessie flushed because she hadn't intended to tell her.

'You are a dark horse! And when did he ask you?'

'This evening, when I opened the bar. He asked me if I would like to go to the pictures. I said I would, but only if we could go Dutch.'

'Now why in heaven's name did you say that? He's been leaning on the counter for months, waiting for the opportunity to ask you.'

'Oh no, he just talks about books and cricket.'

'Oh yes? Still, Cyril said he was one of the nicest fellows in the Depot. Where's he meeting you?'

'At the gate at three-thirty.'

'You should have asked him to call here – just in case you're late.'

On Wednesday morning Jessie was beginning to have second thoughts about her date, but Miss Taylor said she couldn't go back on her word and insisted on lending her kid gloves and handbag. When Pompey arrived at the back door, five minutes before the appointed time, she invited him into the kitchen and engaged him in polite conversation until Jessie was ready.

Eventually they set out for the station. Pompey was completely at ease, chatting as they walked along, but Jessie was tongue-tied and answered in monosyllables. She waited politely, a short distance from the booking office, to allow him to purchase the tickets. It would have been a breach of etiquette to pay for her own, and she had already decided to settle the expenses at the end of the evening. When Pompey rejoined her she was gazing along the railway track.

'A penny for your thoughts.'

'We've missed the train I usually catch. I don't know how long the next one will be.'

'These electric trains run quite frequently. They are a vast improvement on the old locomotives.'

'I didn't know they were electric.'

'You must have noticed there's no engine.'

'No, I'm always late. I just manage to catch the train before it pulls out of the station.'

'I reckon there won't be any steam trains in fifty years time, they'll all be electric.'

'What are volts?'

'Now that's a difficult question. Let's just say that if you touched a live wire on the light in the canteen, you'd have a very nasty shock. If you stepped on a live rail, you'd be dead. It carries hundreds of them.'

The realisation that the signalman had saved her life sent a shudder down Jessie's spine: up to that moment, she had been unaware of the danger.

* * *

186

At Southport the sun was shining and there was a warm breeze. They walked along the seafront until they arrived at Lord Street, where Pompey decided it was time for afternoon tea. Jessie's heart sank when he ushered her into one of the most expensive restaurants on the boulevard. When she had insisted they should go Dutch, she had not bargained for such extravagance.

Realising that Jessie was in a quandary, Pompey took the menu card from her and ordered toasted scones, cakes, and a pot of tea for two. She enjoyed the warm scones, oozing with butter, but when he moved the pedestal of costly cream cakes towards her, she politely refused; he insisted that she should try at least one. She reluctantly took the nearest one, and then diluted the tea with the hot water to pour him a second cup. The pot was still fairly full and it seemed a shame to waste such an expensive brew, so she also had a second cup.

By the time they reached the cinema, Jessie was regretting her canny impulse: she had forgotten to pay a call before she left the canteen and her discomfort was becoming acute. Fortunately, Pompey led the way to the seats, so she was at the end of a row. She had only to think up a suitable excuse in order to retire to the 'Ladies'. When two usherettes came down the aisle, calling out their wares, she stood up quickly, saying, 'Excuse me, I'm just going for some oranges.'

Pompey leapt to his feet. 'All right, I'll...' but before he could finish the sentence, she was half way up the aisle, heading towards the lighted sign.

Her mission accomplished, she groped her way back down the slope, and by the time she reached her seat, the credits were flashing on the screen.

'Did you get the oranges?' whispered Pompey.

'Oh, I forgot.' Her cheeks were burning with embarrassment. However, she consoled herself that her face wasn't visible in the dim light.

It wasn't until they reached the railway station on the return journey that Pompey teased her. 'Excuse me,' he said, with a twinkle in his eye, 'I just want to get some oranges.' He walked briskly towards the gentlemen's toilets.

It was dark when they reached Burscough, but Jessie enjoyed the walk along the country lanes, inhaling the sweet pollen-scented air. On the rare occasions when she returned to the canteen at dusk, she was too busy glancing over her shoulder to appreciate the beauty of her surroundings.

'You're very quiet. Have you enjoyed yourself?'

'Oh yes, thank you. I was just thinking about Stormy. He said I should lock the back door in the evenings.'

'Yes, it's better to be safe than sorry.'

'It's lonely in the lanes but I feel quite safe at the canteen when Stormy's in the cookhouse.'

'You had a good friend in Stormy.'

'Yes, he always gives me good advice.'

'I expect you'll notice the difference now that the regiment is due for service in Egypt.'

'Egypt?'

'Yes, didn't you know?'

'Stormy as well?'

'I expect you'll miss your friend, Paddy Riley.'

Jessie was stunned by the news. She had guessed that Paddy had gone on leave, but it hadn't occurred to her that it was embarkation leave.

Pompey broke the silence, 'I expect you'll miss him teasing you.'

'Yes,' then she added nonchalantly, 'and his blarney.'

By now they had reached the passageway, illuminated by the light over the door of the sergeant's mess. Pompey was serious as he said, 'I wish I'd asked you to come out sooner.'

At the yard door he held out his hand to bid her goodnight.

188

'Goodnight and thank you, Pompey.'

'Scottie, you will come out with me again?'

'Yes, but next time, could we go somewhere not quite so expensive.'

Miss Taylor was waiting in the kitchen and wasn't satisfied until Jessie had recounted every detail. 'You should say, "excuse me", when you go to the ladies.'

'But I didn't want him to know where I was going.'

'Well, next time, just say you're going to powder your nose.'

To change the subject, Jessie enquired if Sergeant Manwaring, the new sergeant, had been in the bar.

'We were very slack. I only took thirty shillings all evening,' was the reticent reply.

'Did you know the battalion is due for service in Egypt?'

'Of course; isn't that why Elaine is rushing Cyril to the altar?'

'Will they close the Depot if the regiment goes abroad?'

'This is a training establishment. Some others will replace the men on the draft.'

'Private Belcher says he's going soon.'

'How old is he?'

'I think he once said he's twenty-eight.'

'Then you want to make the most of your time with him. He's really taken with you. If you marry him, you'll be on the strength.'

'On the strength?'

'Yes, if he's over twenty-six, he would draw an allowance for you and you'd stand a good chance of getting into married quarters.'

'He says he'll be going soon.'

'You were slow. If you'd bucked up your ideas, you could be married by now. You'd have the army allowance. He'd probably make you an allotment as well.'

The manageress was so mercenary, it crossed Jessie's

189

mind that maybe she hadn't been in love with Sergean
Brown: perhaps she just desired the security that the
crown on his sleeve represented.

The following day, half a leg of lamb arrived with the order
Jessie was surprised when the manageress roasted it because
the joint was usually reserved for Sunday dinner. When she
queried the alteration to the normal routine, Miss Taylo
said she thought it would be a good idea to cook the join
mid-week, and they could have the remainder cold on the
following day. When Jessie reminded her that they weren'
supposed to eat meat on Friday, the manageress silenced
her by saying, abruptly, 'We can use it up in the bar.'

Miss Taylor was so unpredictable that Jessie thought nc
more of it until seven-thirty on the same evening, when
the self-opinionated Sergeant Manwaring was giving a
repeat performance of his patter. 'Even you must agree
that the menu is unimaginative, Jock.'

Miss Taylor appeared on the scene, looking unusuall
vivacious in her white overall, worn like the gown of a
Don as a symbol of authority. 'Is anything wrong, Mis
Edmondstone?'

'The sergeant would like more variety on the menu.'

The manageress usually resented any criticism, so Jessi
stood smugly aside, to allow her to cut the sergeant dow
to size with one of her terse remarks. She was astonishe
when Miss Taylor ingratiated herself. 'Would you care fo
cold roast lamb and salad, or perhaps lamb, peas an
potatoes with mint sauce?'

'Cold lamb and salad will do nicely.' The sergean
smirked at Jessie.

'Bread and butter?' Her gentle voice was persuasive.

'Yes please,' said the sergeant, and smiled as their eye
met.

Jock was as astounded as Jessie. He solemnly raised his eyes towards heaven and she badly wanted to laugh.

'It's no' fair, Jock,' she said, as she collected his empty glass. 'That's our dinner she's given to that cocky bloke.'

'It seems to me that there's no beating the system, but some are better at bending the rules than others,' was his reply.

The sergeant continued to put in an occasional appearance in the coffee bar, but Jessie was determined to remain unruffled. In the sergeant's mess, he was probably treated with contempt, but in the men's mess there was more scope for airing his views: he could pull rank on anyone who dared to challenge him. He had now become a regular visitor to the grocery bar therefore it was inevitable that he would receive an invitation to supper. However, Jessie refrained from expressing her disapproval: it was not her place to comment.

Pompey had arranged another visit to Southport on Jessie's next half-day and, once again, Miss Taylor lent her a handbag and gloves, insisting that she must have the correct accessories to be properly dressed. When Pompey arrived, she was pleased she had accepted her superior's advice because he was wearing a smart sports jacket and had sharp creases in his grey flannels. Although he wasn't handsome like Paddy, his pleasant, alert expression made him good-looking.

It was a beautiful day and they stood on the beach to watch the light aircraft as it ploughed through the sand, then soared upwards to circle in the blue sky above. Pompey was keen to take the next flight and Jessie pretended she was nervous: really, it was the cost of five shillings that deterred her. She suggested that they walk to the sea but the soft sand stretched as far as the eye could see and Pompey thought it was hardly worth the effort. Instead, they followed the coastline until they reached the sand dunes, where they stopped to watch the bobbing white tail of a rabbit as it hopped between the tufts of grass.

All too soon, it was time to return to Southport for a delicious meal of plaice and chips, before they took a leisurely stroll to the station. The train wasn't due for fifteen minutes, so they sat in the waiting room to rest their legs. Pompey had read somewhere that Southport pier was built in the 1860s and was the longest in the country until the turn of the century. Although the tides were high in spring, the sea was actually receding and one day, the pier would be marooned on the sand.

As they strolled along the platform, Jessie mused that the conversation had made the time pass quickly. They were just about to board the train when she was seized with panic. Pompey had paused to allow her to enter the compartment ahead of him and, glancing at her, he became very concerned. 'You're as white as a ghost. Do you feel all right?'

'The handbag, I've left it in the waiting room.'

Jessie could feel the colour flooding back into her face as she retrieved the bag, still at the end of the seat where she had left it. Pompey presumed that she was worried about the contents; she didn't enlighten him about the real reason for her anxiety.

Miss Taylor had assured Pompey that it wouldn't matter if they were a little late, but they were back at the Depot by ten forty-five, despite the delay, which had caused them to miss the train.

In the kitchen Jessie found the manageress and Sergeant Manwaring in frivolous mood. They had obviously enjoyed a good supper: the greasy plates and empty Bass bottles were still on the table. Miss Taylor asked her where she had been, but when Jessie started to tell her, the sergeant interposed with his usual flippant remarks, so she shortened her account and wished them both 'Goodnight'.

20

Taking Stock

Jessie's expectation that the manageress would come to her senses was not fulfilled; Sergeant Manwaring was soon ensconced in the leather armchair in the office. Miss Taylor seemed oblivious to his arrogance, hanging on his every word when he boasted about his pub in London and his ten-roomed house in Highgate. When Sergeant Brown had escorted her, she had always observed the rules of etiquette, but now she simpered and gazed into the eyes of her new beau as they strolled out of the Depot, arm in arm. She was so enamoured with him that her mind wasn't on her work. When the September stock-taking came round, the accountant announced a deficit of four pounds.

Mr Ford left no stone unturned, double-checking the contents of the coffee bar and kitchen in his efforts to rectify the mistake. Jessie was quite certain that all unsold food and drinks had been written off and was unable to offer any other explanation to account for the loss. She had worked on the accounts, under the supervision of Sergeant Brown, but had not been asked to continue after he left. It crossed her mind that when he ended the friendship, the manageress didn't realise how many packets of cigarettes she had smoked. It was unlikely that the cost would have been covered by the profit from extra cups of tea, as the men had been drinking shandies during the hot weather.

As soon as Mr Ford departed, Miss Taylor asked Jessie if she was sure she had totted up correctly when she had sold the crates of beer after the cricket final. Gifted with a good memory, Jessie rhymed off the order, which tallied exactly with the entry in the book.

The manageress sighed, 'How I long for the day when I can be free of the worry of the Naafi stock.'

'You won't have to work when you marry Corporal Bowen.' Jessie's remark was intended to console her.

The manageress shrugged. 'As a matter of fact I broke off the engagement last week.'

Jessie noticed, for the first time, that the sapphire and diamond studded engagement ring was no longer on her finger. 'Oh, I'm sorry, I quite liked him.'

'Yes, but you've got to be practical, my girl.' She sat down at the table and searched in her pocket for a cigarette. The packet was empty and, as usual, the door of the grocery was shut, so Jessie was asked to fetch some from the coffee bar. When she returned, the manageress was sitting at the table, pushing back her cuticles. She lit a cigarette and motioned to Jessie to sit down. 'Charles is only twenty-five. It would be different if the gap were on my side.' She drew on her cigarette. 'In any case, he can't afford to keep me. He has to borrow a set of civvies from his pals when he comes to see me.'

'Are you sure you're doing the right thing?'

'I know you don't like Sergeant Manwaring, but you've still got your whole life ahead of you.'

Jessie had become used to her quick changes of mood and wasn't hurt by the rebuff. However, she refrained from expressing her opinion that the manageress was exchanging substance for shadow.

During the next visit of the Area Manager, Jock Craig made it his business to have a confidential chat. Jessie had kept her own counsel, and was unaware that the lance

196

corporal was also dubious about the sergeant's intentions, until she overheard Mr Johnson's comment: 'We cannot deny the girls a little company. After all, we expect them to treat the canteen as their home.'

From the outset, Jessie had taken a dislike to the braggart, but it was not until one particular Saturday evening that he confirmed her suspicion that he was also a scrounger.

The couple came into the kitchen and Miss Taylor went to her room to remove her outdoor clothes.

'Two bottles of Bass, Jock, and a large Capstan.' The sergeant's presumptuous tone annoyed Jessie.

'You do know that I'm not supposed to serve after hours.'

'Oh come now, Molly and I are friends.'

Miss Taylor came into the kitchen.

'What do you fancy, Molly, a Bass or a Guinness?'

'Bring two bottles of Bass, Jessie.'

'And a large Capstan,' added the sergeant with a broad grin on his face.

Jessie fetched the beer and cigarettes, and held out her hand. He fumbled in his trouser pocket, then in his breast pocket, and, finally, found his wallet. 'Can you change a five-pound note?' he enquired, but didn't produce one.

Miss Taylor intervened, 'Leave it Jessie, I'll see that it goes in with your takings.'

Jessie had taken it for granted that the friendship would again be platonic: presumably, he would pay the expenses when they were out; she would settle the bill when they were in. Now, she couldn't help weighing up the situation. Although they went out together at the weekend, supper each evening no longer consisted of cocoa and a sandwich; the manageress also covered the cost of the regular order for Bass and cigarettes.

However, Jessie soon forgot her qualms when Pompey

announced that he had obtained two tickets for a show at the Pier Pavilion on the off-chance that she would be able to accompany him on her half-day. Miss Taylor was full of enthusiasm and fetched her fur necklet to drape round the shoulders of Jessie's plain brown coat. The chain between the beady-eyed head and fluffy tail looked fragile, but the manageress assured her that it was quite strong. However, she refused the offer of matching handbag and gloves, preferring to take her own.

Pompey was determined to make it an evening to remember, and stopped on the boulevard to make a purchase at the Swiss firm, Matti and Tissot. Jessie remonstrated when he presented her with a box of hand-dipped chocolates, but he just laughed and said they would need some sustenance: the Pier Pavilion didn't rise to bacon and eggs.

From the most expensive seats in the house, there was a good view of the stage. Jessie pretended not to notice Pompey's sidelong glances when the chorus of beautiful girls gave a polished performance of high kicks, displaying more of their skimpy underwear than was decent.

The opening scenes of the comedy were rather far-fetched, but they laughed when the leading man had affairs with three different girls in quick succession. They were particularly amused when the lodger was given sausage and bacon while the husband had to make do with bacon and egg.

The performance was over in two hours and, despite the coolness of the October evening, people were sauntering under the verandas and looking in the lighted shop windows. Jessie refused the offer of a drink because she wasn't sure if the invitation was to a public house; in any case, she didn't want to be back late.

It was not until they reached the yard door that Pompey imparted the news that it was his turn to go on leave.

Jessie asked, 'Will I see you before you go to Egypt?'

'I hope so. If I can't see you before I go, I'll write to you as soon as I disembark.' He shook her hand and hesitated. Jessie stretched up and kissed him lightly on the cheek.

Miss Taylor was waiting in the kitchen, to re-live every moment of the evening. When Jessie told her she really wanted to buy Pompey a present before he went on leave, she commented, 'One of these days you'll learn some sense, my girl. Use what you save to buy yourself a smart outfit, then they'll all be falling over themselves to take you out.'

'Oh, I couldn't do that.'

'If they don't spend their pay on you, they'll only treat some other girl.'

The following Wednesday, a mist hung over the tree tops when Jessie set out for Southport, so she didn't linger. She returned early to the Depot and found Sergeant Manwaring standing in the kitchen with his arm around Miss Taylor. Jessie refused the offer of tea and went to her bedroom to inspect her purchase: two lace-trimmed under sets.

After the last stock-taking, Miss Taylor had predicted that the Naafi wouldn't allow too much time to elapse before the next one, and she was right: it was scarcely a month and Mr Ford was due to come again.

It was now the end of October and the chill nip in the air had resulted in an increased demand for hot cups of tea. Jessie had made an extra half-gallon every dinner time and was confident that, this time, the accountant would be satisfied.

Mr Ford checked and double-checked the stock. It was after six o'clock when he finally departed, still unable to account for another loss of four pounds. Miss Taylor was morose. She told Jessie that the Area Manager would probably pay them a visit, and then retired to the office. The next day she filled every ashtray in the canteen with cigarette stubs, but the expected visit didn't take place.

On Wednesday morning, Mr Johnson arrived, at last, and was taken straight to the office. After some time, he came into the kitchen and placed some papers on the table. 'This is the second time the stock has been down by four pounds. Can you account for the discrepancy?'

Jessie found it difficult to analyse the figures on the sheet. The last entry was three pounds, five shillings and six pence, but there should have been an extra shilling for Bass and cigarettes. She was still trying to fathom how this mistake had occurred when Mr Johnson picked up the papers. 'I shall have to send you to London ... otherwise...'

London! All thoughts about the missing money went completely out of Jessie's head. She was vaguely aware that the Area Manager was still speaking to her, but she was so entranced by the thought of a transfer to the capital that his words failed to register in her brain. She would be near John. It would make her mother so happy when she received news of her eldest son.

Mr Johnson's solemn face came back into focus. 'I'll write out the directions and leave the warrant with Miss Taylor.'

The Area Manager went into the bar and spoke to Jock Craig, but the subject of their discussion was of no interest to Jessie. She was so elated she could hardly contain herself.

As soon as Mr Johnson departed, she went to impart

the news: 'Corporal Craig, I'm going to London, isn't it wonderful?'

'Do you really want to leave here? I can sort this mess out, you know.'

'My brother's on boy service in the Guards and I haven't seen him for at least two years. It will be lovely to be near him. He's only sixteen.'

'You are quite sure you want to go?'

'Oh yes, corporal, I'll probably never get the chance again.'

Jock looked concerned. After a pause, his voice was husky. 'I hope you get on all right, but if there are any problems, just let me know.'

The news of Jessie's transfer quickly circulated. She was quite moved when several of the men came to the counter to wish her 'all the best'.

Before she put up the last shutter, she turned to thank her self-appointed mentor, but he must have slipped away: he was not in his usual place at the end of the counter.

It was convenient that the transfer was arranged for Jessie's half-day: she was free to give her bedroom a special clean. By the evening she had packed her suitcase, and asked for the address of Imperial Court in order to write the labels. Miss Taylor advised her to travel light and volunteered to forward her luggage as soon as she heard from her.

By the time Jessie fell into bed, her usually sound judgement had been impaired by fatigue. Perhaps she should have drawn the attention of Mr Johnson to the error on the statement, but one shilling would have made little difference to the total. Apparently, the extra tea had not offset the losses in the grocery, but the Naafi's profits were not her problem; her own financial state was more a cause for concern.

During the heat wave, Miss Taylor had advised her that artificial silk was cooler under the Naafi overall and there was the added advantage that the fine fabric would dry quickly in winter. She now regretted the unnecessary expenditure, which had left her with only twenty-five shillings. However, the Naafi was a good employer and would provide for all her needs. Her training would stand her in good stead and perhaps she would soon be promoted to charge hand...

The following morning Jessie was up early and cleaned the stove for the last time. Miss Taylor insisted that she must have a cooked breakfast, but her own bacon and egg remained untouched while, deep in thought, she smoked a cigarette.

In the scullery, Jessie washed up the dishes and wondered if Miss Taylor would have to manage on her own until the next cohort arrived. However, there was no time for further speculation: she must be at Lime Street in plenty of time to catch her connection.

Having collected her parcel of possessions from the bedroom, she tearfully kissed Miss Taylor goodbye. She had come to regard the manageress as a maiden aunt, rather than her superior, and was sorry to leave her without an assistant. The manageress showed little emotion. Her parting words were, 'When you reach your next canteen, don't forget to send me your address and I'll send your luggage on.'

21

Imperial Court

Jessie's journey in the 'Ladies Only' compartment of a fast train to London was uneventful. It was dinner time when she arrived at Euston, but the refreshments in the tearoom would probably be expensive, so she continued on her way to Euston Square; then caught an underground train to Kennington. The instructions to walk south were quite straightforward, but it was difficult to identify the buildings, set back from the main road. However, a passer-by was very helpful: 'The headquarters of the Naafi is a large building with two gates and iron railings.'

When Jessie arrived at Imperial Court she was unable to open the first gate but, further along, there was a hut behind the railings. As she approached the second gate, she could see that the upper half of the hut door was open; the man inside was wearing a blue uniform and had an ex-serviceman's badge on his lapel. He glanced at the name on her letter of introduction, made a brief telephone call and sent her to the main entrance. She was just about to push open one of the double swing doors when a lady emerged and enquired if she was Miss Edmondstone. 'Come inside, and take off your coat. I'm afraid you are too late for lunch, but would you care for egg and chips?'

Left alone, Jessie sat looking around at the small vases of flowers on the green-topped tables. The large room resembled a high-class restaurant, except that the meals were probably served at the counter. Although it was a dull day, the freshly decorated walls and large windows made the room light and airy. Any doubts about her hasty transfer were dispelled: the facilities were obviously much better than those at Burscough.

The lady reappeared with a white place mat, condiments and a plate of bread and butter; then went back through the door beside the counter to fetch a poached egg, already served on a plate, and a generous portion of chips on an oblong white dish.

Jessie enjoyed the meal, which had been cooked to perfection. When she was offered tea and cakes, she politely refused.

'If you've finished, I'll give you the directions to your new canteen.' The lady produced a piece of paper from her pocket. 'Return to Kennington Station and take the train to London Bridge. You may have to wait for the next train to Gravesend, but they are fairly frequent.'

Jessie was so stunned that she didn't hear the last of the instructions, but they were written on the paper, so she mumbled her thanks and was shown out of the building. She had been under the impression that she would be staying in London and had never heard of Gravesend, which must be some distance away if she had to catch another steam train.

At London Bridge, she enquired the times of the train and was told that she would have to wait for half an hour so she decided to venture outside the station.

An elderly flower-seller stopped clearing her pitch when Jessie approached. She had never heard of Birdcage Walk but an old man, smoking a clay pipe, overheard the conversation. 'Are you sure it's round these parts?'

'I don't know, my brother is in the Scots Guards at Wellington Barracks.'

'There's only one Birdcage Walk that I knows of, up near the Palace.'

'Is it far?'

He sucked his pipe and looked up at the sky. 'Looks like we're in fer a pea-souper. Yer best bet is ter 'op on a bus and arsk when yer get to Trafalgar Square.' He then added that he had a few minutes to spare, so he would show her the bus stop.

Jessie had presumed that Wellington Barracks would be within walking distance and had no intention of making another journey, but she was pleased to stretch her legs. They came to the bus stop, just as the bus arrived; the old man obligingly asked the conductor to make sure she got off at the right stop as he ushered her on to the platform.

At Trafalgar Square, the people were anxious to be on their way as the fog began to descend. When Jessie asked for directions, their instructions were very brief: 'Go through the arch', 'It's on the other side of the park', 'Turn left at the fountain'.

Jessie had no difficulty in finding Admiralty Arch, but when she reached St James Park, visibility was down to a few yards. However, she thought she had almost reached her destination and set off at a steady pace to follow the path. As the fog became denser, she stopped to listen for the sound of traffic, but she couldn't see or hear anything: the silence was un-nerving. The loud chimes of a clock reminded her that she was supposed to be on the train to Gravesend. However, she continued on her way, distracted by her recollection of the final events at Burscough. Miss Taylor had been evasive when she had requested the address of Imperial Court. Her parting instructions were to send her new address, so she must have known that her next job wasn't in London. If she hadn't asked for directions at Kennington, she wouldn't have found out that Imperial Court was the headquarters of the Naafi.

Preoccupied by her thoughts, Jessie had strayed off the path. As she stood, engulfed in fog, shivering and alone on the wet grass, she was gripped with fear. Someone whistled and called, 'Nell, Nell.' A dog ran past. She quickly pulled herself together and followed the direction the dog had taken. Eventually, she stumbled back on to the path and concentrated on following it, stopping occasionally to peer through the blanket of fog. It seemed as if she had walked a very long way before she saw a faint glimmer of light, and hurried towards the beam, which was wavering up and down. When she was just able to discern the dark outline of a policeman's helmet, she rushed towards him and grabbed his arm.

'Steady there,' he said, and shone his torch on her face.

'I'm lost and I'm trying to find Wellington Barracks.' The tears were rolling down her cheeks.

The policeman listened patiently while Jessie explained her predicament and then said, kindly, 'Don't worry, I'll show you the way.'

Eventually, they reached the edge of a roadway. 'It's not far now,' he said, 'the barracks are on the other side of the road. Are you sure your brother will be there?'

'Oh, yes,' said Jessie, but as she walked warily across the road, she wasn't so sure. What if he had been transferred to another depot? If the guard refused to admit her, how would she find her way back to the station? It was too late now to turn back.

At the gate of the barracks, she asked the tall guardsman on sentry duty, 'Please could I speak to my brother?'

The guard's lips moved. 'Which regiment?'

'The Scots Guards.'

'This is the Irish Guards, not the next gate, try the third one. The Scots are in there.'

At the third gate Jessie's voice faltered as she addressed the tall sentry, who replied, 'Ask at the hut behind me

She knocked on the door, which was slightly ajar.

'Yes, what do you want?'

'Could I speak to my wee brother? He's on boy service.'

'What's your name and where do you live?'

The sergeant was evidently satisfied when she gave her mother's name and home address and went back inside to dispatch another incumbent. A head appeared round the door to catch a glimpse of the diminutive big sister; then there were loud guffaws inside the hut.

Jessie hadn't seen John since he boarded the train at Aberdeen to return to Dunblane, dressed in a khaki jacket, tartan kilt and Glengarry. She didn't recognise the tall young man in a canvas suit, who had been summoned, until he said, 'Jessie! What are you doing here?'

'I changed my job. I had a few hours to spare.'

'Wait here while I get changed.'

When John returned, dressed in uniform, he said that Jessie was lucky to catch him: he had been swimming and had just made up his mind to go out for the evening. His friend had been invited to tea with some rich old boy, and wanted him to go with him. Jessie was concerned that she had upset his arrangements but he said that he had been undecided and to forget it.

Westminster, on a foggy night, was not the best time to go sightseeing. Jessie asked if there was somewhere they could go to have a snack, and gave him two half-crowns.

In a café, owned by an ex-guardsman, Jessie sat at a table while John fetched two large cups of tea and two thick sandwiches. He explained that Sam had asked him how he had managed to find himself a rich girlfriend: hence the incredulous laughter.

Jessie began by recounting the events leading up to her recruitment by the Naafi. Father was pleased that he had been instrumental in finding her employment; he was also convinced that he had acted in John's best interests by signing him up for a career. Mam was heartbroken that the transfer had been arranged without her knowledge and now she was upset that her efforts to make amends by sending him some pocket money, were continually being frustrated.

The fog had lifted slightly and John suggested a visit to Westminster Abbey, but Jessie's friend in Aberdeen had enthused about the new Catholic Cathedral. He shrugged. 'No problem, if that's where you'd like to go.'

At the Cathedral, John waited outside while Jessie made a quick visit. When she came out, she commented that she wasn't surprised that John didn't want to go in. The fog, swirling round the crucifix, had added to the gloom of the bare bricks of the unfinished interior.

'It's not the building. I hate passing the man at the door, holding the plate.'

'I didn't have any change, so I just walked by.'

'One day they'll erect a commemorative plaque made of trouser buttons. We're all broke before church parade on Sunday. The metal clinks like a coin when it's dropped into the collection.'

John knew a short cut to the station but, first, Jessie must come back to the barracks because he wanted her to have an assortment of prizes he had won for swimming. She explained that it was unlikely there would be any storage space at Gravesend and, in any case, she wasn't sure how long she would be staying there.

At London Bridge as the train was about to depart, Jessie quickly made a parting plea. 'Please write to Mam. Christmas is coming and that pewter fruit bowl, and all the other things, would make her the proudest woman in Carlisle.'

John didn't reply. He put his hand over the barrier to

pat her arm; then turned away. She fought back the tears and tried to swallow the lump in her throat as she waited for him to wave, but he didn't look back as he marched quickly towards the exit.

'If you want this train, miss, you'd better get a move on.' The guard opened the door of an empty compartment and, with a sigh of relief, Jessie climbed in.

On the short journey, Jessie anticipated a cool reception at her next canteen, but there was little her superiors could do except, perhaps, cancel her half-day.

22

Under Suspicion

'This is Milton Barracks.' The elderly lady pointed to the opening between the pillars of a high brick wall.

Jessie peered through the entrance, but the dense October mist had reduced visibility inside the enclosure to a few yards. Catching sight of a sentry box, she breathed a sigh of relief: although her destination was a fairly short walk from Gravesend Station, she could easily have lost her way in the dimly lit, deserted streets. She turned to express her gratitude, but the Good Samaritan had already disappeared into the darkness.

The wet vapour caused Jessie to shiver as she walked through the open, wrought iron gates and waited at the entry box. It was too dark to see inside, but it appeared to be unoccupied. She decided to ask for directions at the barracks, and set off towards the opposite side of the forecourt, but when she continued to walk straight ahead, she realised she was on a roadway. By now, she could just discern the dim outline of buildings, and veered towards a shaft of light at the far end.

A figure came jogging out of the darkness.

'Excuse me, could you direct me to the Naafi?' Jessie's voice sounded muffled, but the young man, clutching a metal plate and cutlery, stopped in his tracks.

'The canteen or the staff quarters?'

'The staff quarters, please.'

'Are you coming to work here?'

'Yes.'

'The lads will be pleased. If we want a meal, we have to bring our own plates. Then we have to wash them up.'

The soldier escorted Jessie past the lighted windows of the canteen and into a small passage with a solid wooden door at each side. With clenched fist, he gave a sharp rap on the door to the left. There was no reply, so he advised her to walk straight in.

Left alone, Jessie knocked again and waited; then turned the handle and looked round the door, not knowing what to expect.

A cook was standing beside the range at the far side of a spacious kitchen. She glanced round and asked abruptly, 'What do you want?'

At that moment, the door at the opposite side of the passage was opened by a woman, wearing a navy blue skirt and white satin blouse. Jessie recognised the usual attire of a manageress and held out her letter of introduction saying, 'I have to report to Miss Kitney.'

Probably in her early thirties, the manageress was slim and quite attractive, despite the red rims round her eyes. She tore open the envelope with nicotine-stained fingers. Having perused the contents, she called across the kitchen, 'Cook, this is your new kitchen maid.'

'I'm not a kitchen maid,' said Jessie, indignantly.

Without a pause for breath, the manageress replied, 'Nothing to do with me. See the supervisor when she comes. I understood you would be here at half past four.'

'I was delayed by the fog.'

'I'm much too busy to go up the yard and find you an overall.' She glared across the kitchen. 'Cook, find your kitchen maid an apron.'

Cook raised an eyebrow, and slowly responded by rummaging through several untidy drawers. She tossed a creased apron over the table; then started to pour gravy over the sausages on a metal plate.

Jessie looked around for somewhere to hang her coat and noticed a row of four chairs under the windows, along one side of the room. She placed her felt hat and bag on one, and draped her wet gabardine over the back. Having examined the dirty apron, she put it on with the cleanest side next to her best brown serge dress, and stood beside the table.

The cook was probably about the same age as the manageress but her care-worn face and miserable demeanour gave the impression that she was much older. 'It's at least a month since I had a kitchen maid,' she said, mournfully.

'Well, what would you like me to do?'

'You could peel three pounds of potatoes.' She nodded towards a door near the end of a painted wall. 'The scales are in the larder.'

It was obvious that the kitchen cleaning had been neglected, but Jessie was appalled when she switched on the light and found the small room in such disarray. On the cluttered shelves there were utensils, jars, and torn paper bags of ingredients. The floor was strewn with earth and empty potato sacks; in the corner there were four large cabbages, pungent and yellow with age. Hanging on the wall there were three large iron frying pans, each with a stalactite of congealed fat suspended below it.

Jessie concentrated on extracting some potatoes from a full sack, and was about to weigh them when she discovered that the pan on the brass scales was coated with earth. On the shelf there was a dirty knife, which she used as a scraper, but the surface was caked with dried mud, so she gave up, and resorted to guesswork.

Back in the kitchen, cook produced a peeler and pointed to a large iron saucepan on the shelf above the sink. By the time Jessie had cleaned off the scum round the rim, and peeled the potatoes, a large pile of cooking utensils had been stacked on the draining board.

Cook stopped wiping the kitchen table to give the next instruction: 'Miss Kitney and Mrs Williams will be here soon. Put the kettle on the gas ring before you start on the dishes.'

The washing up had almost been completed when the manageress and charge hand arrived, pulled two of the chairs to one end of the long kitchen table and sat, puffing their cigarettes.

Jessie fetched a chair for cook, who placed it at the other end of the table and, having poured the tea, sat down to read her newspaper. With her wet gabardine, turned inside out over her knees, Jessie sat down beside her.

After a while, cook remembered she now had an assistant and pushed a plate of rock cakes towards her. Jessie was hungry, but the rock cake lived up to its name; she was relieved when there was no offer of another.

Eventually, the charge hand broke the silence. 'Come along, I'll show you to the staff quarters.'

By the time that Jessie had replaced her chair, and picked up her belongings, Mrs Williams was holding open the door, leading to an open area between the canteen and the brick wall of another building. The contrast between the heat of the kitchen and the cold night air caused her teeth to chatter as she followed the charge hand up the yard, lit by the kitchen windows, and climbed an iron staircase, alongside the wall.

On the landing, Mrs Williams fumbled in her pocket for the keys to unlock the door, which opened into a passage. She stopped to collect an overall and a towel from a linen cupboard; then switched on the light in a gloomy bedroom, saying, 'Each morning you will bring three cups of tea: one for the manageress, one for cook and one for me.' Pointing to two open drawers in a chest, he continued, 'Those are for you. The keys are there so hey can be locked. I've wound the alarm. You must be outside the canteen door at seven-thirty. Gwennie will be here with the keys.'

Left alone, Jessie hung her damp gabardine in the cupboard and placed her bag on the chest of drawers. She was still shivering, so she decided to wear her nightdress over her underclothes. It was obvious that the bed linen had not been changed after the previous occupant vacated the room, but it was too late to request clean sheets.

The room was pitch black as Jessie groped her way from he light switch to the iron bedstead. She tried to settle down under the musty covers and ignore the pillow, which reeked of stale tobacco, but the turmoil in her brain prevented her from falling asleep. Why had she been transferred to this dirty canteen as a kitchen maid? Perhaps t was just a temporary arrangement because the Naafi was so short of staff. She rubbed her legs in an effort to restore he circulation, but her feet still felt like blocks of ice. As she tossed and turned, she recalled that when the Area Manager had asked her if she could explain the large deficit, he had shown her the accounts for the coffee bar. She checked and re-checked her mental arithmetic: approximately five extra cups of tea per day would have made a profit of twelve shillings by the end of a month. This would easily cover the cost of a carton of cigarettes, added to the coffee bar account, but sold in the grocery.

The pillow was soon saturated with Jessie's tears of frustration and self-pity. If only she had kept her savings intact, she would now have the fare home to Carlisle. She would have to remain at this dirty canteen for the time being, but she had learnt her lesson: on no account would she deviate from the Naafi rules in future.

* * *

215

A bugle sounded the reveille. Jessie groped her way across the room to switch on the light. It was only six o'clock. She went back to bed and had just begun to doze when the alarm rang.

The washbasin was dirty, so she ran the tap to splash cold water on her puffy eyes. Having wound her plait into a bun, she draped her gabardine round her shoulders then remembered to lock her handbag in the drawer before she descended into the dark, misty yard, to wait outside the kitchen.

It was not long before a girl appeared. 'I'm Gwennie. What's your name?'

'Jessie.'

Gwennie unlocked the two doors and switched on the light. 'You look as if you've been crying. Are you homesick?'

'No, I was looking forward to being near my brother. I didn't know I was coming here as a kitchen maid.'

'I'll soon have the fire alight. If you put the kettle on the gas, we can have a cup of tea.'

When the coal had started to glow, the pretty, brown haired girl took a tray up to the rest of the staff, and then rejoined Jessie in the kitchen. As they drank their tea she enquired, 'Didn't you have any training before you came here?'

'Yes, I went to Bury for a month's training to be a general assistant.'

'And they sent you here as a kitchen maid?'

'The Naafi moves people around, so when the Area Manager said I would have to go to London, I just thought they needed a general assistant at another canteen.'

'I'm glad my father wouldn't let me sign up for the Naafi.'

'But you work here?'

'I'm in charge of the coffee bar. Miss Kitney asked me to come early to show you what to do. They'll all be here soon, so we'd better get a move on.'

Gwennie washed their teacups; then helped Jessie to lay the table.

Cook was the first to arrive and started to fry bacon and eggs, complaining that she hadn't had a kitchen maid for a month and her leg was bad this morning.

During breakfast it was Gwennie who started the conversation by asking how long it would be before the regiment returned from manoeuvres, because she wanted to make sure her bar was well stocked. Miss Kitney and Mrs Williams ignored her question, showing no interest in the whereabouts of the regiment as they smoked their cigarettes. Cook said that extra suppers would be required and it was a good job she now had a kitchen maid.

The brief conversation ended when Gwennie stood up and said to Jessie, 'See you at dinner time.' Her departure seemed to remind the manageress and charge hand that it was time to stub out their cigarettes.

After breakfast, Jessie washed up, then asked if she should start on the larder.

Cook said, 'Yes, but don't forget it's your job to do the bedrooms.'

After a while, she came to see how her new assistant was getting on. By then, Jessie had folded the potato sacks into a neat pile, swept the floor, and managed to wipe the grease off the wall without removing all the whitewash. Cook decided that one of the four rotting cabbages could be salvaged for the dinner. The best way to dispose of the other three was to chop them up small and mix them with earth in a bucket, but the bedrooms would have to be done first.

Mrs Williams and Miss Kitney came into the kitchen, which gave Jessie the opportunity to ask for clean sheets. The charge hand apologised for the oversight, but the manageress remarked that if she had managed to arrive on time, she would have received not only sheets, but also an overall.

After they had departed, cook said irritably, 'I do wish they'd take these trays into the coffee bar.' The trays of rock cakes were taking up space on the dresser, so Jessie volunteered to take them through. It took only a few seconds to transfer the first tray to a table in the bar on the other side of the passage. As she retraced her steps, the manageress came behind her. 'Your place is in the kitchen. On no account must you enter the coffee bar.' She picked up the second tray of cakes and said in a dictatorial voice, 'Cook, did you hear what I said?'

'Yes, I heard.' The reply was spoken in a disinterested drawl.

The realisation that the manageress thought she was a thief, caused Jessie to burst into tears. Cook limped across the kitchen and said quietly, 'Take no notice of her. Make a start upstairs. A walk in the fresh air will do you good.'

Mrs Williams was in her bedroom and provided clean bed linen, with the comment, 'You are stopping!'

'I don't know. I'll have to wait for my luggage and see the supervisor.'

Jessie set to work to brush the mats. Having swept one room, she tried to move the bed in the next room, but it was too heavy. She covered the head of the broom with a duster and was using it to remove the layer of fluff and feathers when the clink of metal aroused her curiosity. To her surprise, a florin and a half crown slid out from under the bed, but there was nothing else.

Mrs Williams was still in her bedroom and appeared to be washing her underwear. She asked if the other rooms had been cleaned, then said to leave hers until the next day.

In the kitchen, cook was rolling pastry and enquired if Jessie felt better now. 'I'd make us a cup of tea, but it's almost dinner time. Now don't wear out all my saucepans. Fill them with water and put them under the sink. It will make the job easier for you.'

On the second morning Gwennie and Jessie arrived together and unlocked the doors. Gwennie supervised the preparation of the staff tea and lit the fire. Jessie braved the cold wind and shakily mounted the iron staircase to place the tray outside the charge hand's bedroom door. As Gwennie had jobs to do in her own bar, she left Jessie to lay the table while cook fried bacon and eggs.

After breakfast, the dishes were soon washed up, and Jessie was about to scrub the slimy draining board, when cook said, 'My leg is really bad this morning,' and sat down on a chair.

Jessie looked at her ashen face and was concerned. 'Would you like me to prepare the vegetables for you?'

'No, just carry on. I'll be all right in a minute. Spread the sacks out in the larder. The concrete is so cold under my feet.'

Having obliged, Jessie returned to the kitchen to help to prepare the beef casserole and peel the apples for the plate apple tart.

After dinner, Jessie asked Gwennie if she sold writing paper in her bar. She replied that she collected anything she needed from the coffee bar: she couldn't keep much stock because the corporal's bar was small.

'Would you get me a writing pad, two envelopes and two stamps please?'

'Why can't you get them yourself?'

'I'm not allowed to go in there.'

'Why not?'

'There were two bad stocks before I left Burscough. There were only two of us, and it looks as if I'm the one under suspicion.'

Gwennie fetched the stationery. As Jessie's hands were wet, she put it on the dresser with her change from half a crown.

By two-thirty, cook was off duty and the kitchen was

almost tidy when Miss Kitney came in and spotted the money on the dresser. 'Who left that on there?'

Jessie explained that it was her change from the writing paper and stamps.

'Where did you find the money?'

'In my purse.'

'How much was it?'

'Half a crown.'

'On the floor?'

'Oh, you mean that money! I put the half crown and florin under the pillow.'

'Which pillow?'

'I don't know whose bed it was. It was in the room where I found it.'

The manageress snorted and went into the yard. As she walked past the windows towards the iron staircase, Jessie came to the conclusion that the coins had been deliberately placed under the bed to test her honesty. It seemed as if the Naafi couldn't produce any evidence to sack her; she had been sent to a dirty canteen to encourage her to give in her notice. The injustice strengthened her resolve. She sat down at the table and composed a brief letter to let Miss Taylor know where to send her luggage. She also mentioned that she was working hard because cook had not had a kitchen maid for a month, but she was now settling into the new routine.

23

Manoeuvres

On her third day at the Barracks, Jessie was awakened by the reveille and arrived in the kitchen, ready to follow her usual routine. On the previous evening, the manageress had informed her that, as Gwennie wouldn't be coming early, the keys to the kitchen would be outside her bedroom door.

It took longer than usual to clear the clogged flues using a poker: there was an old flue brush in the corner of the larder, but there didn't appear to be a rake. However, the firewood kindled quickly, and the layer of soot on the congoleum was scarcely visible: the floor was already black with dirt.

Mrs Williams was the first to appear. 'You forgot to bring the morning tea.'

'Oh, I'm sorry. Is it too late now?'

'I suppose so.' She went out into the passage, heaving a sigh as she closed the door.

By the time the manageress arrived, Jessie had wiped the table and washed her face at the kitchen sink. Miss Kitney made no comment and went to join the charge hand in the coffee bar.

Cook had overslept and limped into the kitchen, so concerned that the breakfast would be late that she didn't appear to notice the sooty atmosphere. She produced a toasting fork and told Jessie to make five slices of toast while she scrambled the eggs.

After breakfast, Jessie started to fill a bucket to wash the soot off the congoleum near the hearth, but cook said it would be more sensible to make a start upstairs because she was about to weigh up. The bedrooms had been swept the previous day, so it didn't take long to dust the furniture and clean the washbasins. As there didn't appear to be a bathroom, the daily cleaning of the staff quarters would be a good opportunity to have a wash.

Feeling refreshed, and in a much happier frame of mind, Jessie walked back along the yard. At the kitchen door, she was confronted by the cook, brandishing her rolling pin. 'It's all your fault,' she shouted. 'You shouldn't have done it.'

On the table there were two trays of rock cakes, burnt so black that it would be impossible to salvage them. Jessie was about to protest her innocence when the manageress asked, 'Did you clean the range this morning?'

'Yes at Burscough I cleaned the range every morning.'

'This isn't Burscough. In future, don't do anything without asking first. All these cakes will have to be written off.'

'I'm sorry. I'll pay for them.'

'You will not!' Miss Kitney flounced out of the kitchen.

Jessie volunteered to weigh the ingredients for another batch. Cook ignored the offer and picked up the coal-scuttle.

'Please don't put any more coal on the fire. At Bury, there was a mark on the firebrick and we had to make sure the coal didn't go above it.'

Cook said huffily, 'Oh well, as you know what to do, you'd better make up the fire. The coal is in the shed under the iron staircase, the door next to the toilet.'

As Jessie shovelled the coal, she mused that she had inadvertently done herself a favour. If she didn't have to clean the range every morning, her one change of underwear would last until her suitcase arrived.

On her return to the kitchen, cook was less hostile. 'Mrs Williams has found you a clean overall. It will save time if you put it on in the larder.'

Jessie weighed and rubbed in the dry ingredients; cook added a little extra flour for good measure and then mixed in the egg. Baked at the correct temperature, the rock cakes were a vast improvement. When Mrs Williams requested another batch, Jessie was pleased to leave what she was doing to assist.

At three o'clock Jessie should have been off duty, but she stayed in the kitchen to scrub a section of the floor. Cook was unrolling the bandage on her leg and said, 'Leave that, just sit down and have a break. I must change this dressing.'

Jessie stopped work in case she could be of assistance, but the sight of the ulcerated leg caused her to feel faint. She could hear cook's agitated voice in the distance: 'Sit down, for heaven's sake, don't chuck a dummy on me. Put your head down. I'll have to get someone.'

As her eyes began to focus, Jessie pulled herself together. 'I'm all right now. I just can't stand the sight of blood.'

'You shouldn't be working in a kitchen if you have these turns. What if you'd fallen on the stove?'

'I didn't realise your leg was so bad. I'll be all right.'

'Your colour is coming back. I'll make you a cup of tea.'

While she was waiting for the kettle to boil, cook mentioned that she had joined the Naafi because she only had a small pension after her husband died. Her eyes filled with tears as she explained that Mr Miles had been gassed in the trenches. Having nursed him to the end, she couldn't bear to be alone in the house with so many unhappy memories.

Jessie's sympathy for Mrs Miles helped to divert her attention from her own plight. During the next few days, she made slow progress with the cleaning because she was also acting as assistant cook, but it didn't seem to matter.

Around seven o'clock one evening, a young soldier knocked on the kitchen door with a message for the manageress: the girl in the corporal's bar needs someone to serve while she's making the tea. As the situation in the kitchen was obviously well under control, Miss Kitney said, 'Cook, I think you can manage. Jessie had better go across and give a hand.'

Gwennie was relieved when her friend arrived. 'Thank goodness you've come. Look at the length of the queue!'

Jessie helped to brew and pour the tea until the rush was over; then they both sat down to wait for the next onslaught. It wasn't long before two more soldiers arrived. Gwennie served the first one while Jessie poured a cup of tea for the second. As he turned towards his companion, she noticed the two badges on his cap. 'I hope you won't think I'm rude, but why have you a badge on the back of your cap as well as the front?'

The corporal replied, 'The Gloucesters are the only regiment to have this honour. It dates back to 1801 when the men fought back to back at Alexandria.'

The arrival of some more of his friends ended the brief conversation.

Jessie sat down again, saying, 'I feel awful sitting here while cook is struggling.'

'All right, I think most of the rush is over now. I don't know why you're worrying, but you can go back if you like.'

Back in the kitchen, there was no sign of Mrs Miles. The manageress was lifting a pot of potatoes to transfer a spoonful to a plate. She repeated the process with the peas; then took the plate to the range to ladle gravy over the sausages.

Mrs Williams rushed in. 'It's bedlam in there. Where's cook?'

'She's walked out, just typical, no consideration.'

Simmering on the stove was a large pot of potatoes. Jessie divided them between two saucepans and placed them on the gas rings. Next, she prepared two trays of sausages and placed them in the hot oven.

The flustered charge hand came in and stood at the table, becoming increasingly agitated as she waited for the next meal to be served in slow motion.

'Would you like me to serve some suppers?' Jessie enquired, expecting to be put in her place.

The manageress replied, 'Do you think you can manage?'

Jessie poured the gravy into a jug and transferred three plates from the rack to the table. With a large spoon, she quickly served the sausages, potatoes and peas and added the gravy. The charge hand grabbed the plates and rushed back into the bar. Each time she returned, the next three plates were ready.

As the potatoes on the gas rings were already half cooked, there was only a slight delay while Jessie mashed them with butter and milk.

The bar closed at nine-thirty. Mrs Williams flopped down on a kitchen chair, saying, 'I must have a cigarette.'

She looked so weary that Jessie asked if she would like a cup of tea.

'Yes, but I must check up first. I don't know how we're going to manage without a cook. We've used up all the eatables.'

When she next came into the kitchen, she gave Jessie

two biscuits and apologised: it hadn't occurred to her that they would need something for supper when she sold the last of the biscuits. There was no food left in the larder and just enough milk for three cups of tea.

The next morning, Jessie prepared the tray of tea for two and took it up. The milk and bread had been delivered but she was at a loss to know what to do about breakfast. However, Gwennie had received a message to come early and said that the staff would have to make do with toast.

When Miss Kitney and Mrs Williams arrived, they lit their cigarettes and pondered upon the problem of re stocking the bars. Gwennie was sent to the local bakery for four dozen cakes, at a penny each, and two dozen others, but they must cost no more than three ha'pence each. She soon returned empty-handed and said that, even if the baker had received a special order on the previous day, he couldn't supply cakes at that price.

The manageress and charge hand sat at the kitchen table in a quandary, drawing hard on their cigarettes. The last contingent was due back in the evening, but everything would be back to normal on the following day, when the soldiers would have their meals in the army dining room. Jessie knew that she could easily make six dozen cakes but she was deterred by her suspicion that the coins under the bed had been placed there as a temptation: anyone who could do such a mean trick didn't deserve any favours. Her thoughts turned to the corporal with the badge on the back of his cap. If she didn't volunteer, it was the soldiers who would go hungry. She hesitated. 'I could make some rock cakes.'

Miss Kitney looked sceptical but Mrs Williams said, 'One batch would be better than nothing.'

Gwennie had no wish to wander round Gravesend on

226

a cold day, trying to find a baker who would oblige, so she said quickly, 'I'll help you.'

Two trays of rock cakes were produced in record time but, by then, it was after eleven. Gwennie suggested that Jessie could make some cheese sandwiches ready for the evening rush; the staff could also have some for dinner.

Left alone in the kitchen, Jessie was about to transfer the regular order for meat and vegetables to the larder, but decided that the pork chops should be cooked straight away.

At dinner time she was amused at the amazement on the faces of the staff as she served pork chops, roast potatoes and carrots, followed by baked apples and custard. Gwennie commented that all the rock buns had been snapped up, and added, 'My corporals send you their regards.'

There was now no sign of a replacement for the cook but, otherwise, the canteen was nearly back to normal. Gwennie had agreed to arrive early each day to help Jessie to prepare dinner for the staff, and suppers to serve in the coffee bar.

Jessie's triumph was short lived. A batch of rock cakes was cooling on a tray when the manageress happened to come into the kitchen. She picked one up. 'These are much too big. Cook always made a lot more.'

'I'm using the quantities in the Naafi recipe book.'

'But you aren't allowing for breakages.'

'The rules are an extra two on each batch. If you want to check when I'm weighing up...'

'I have more important things to do than watch an amateur cook!'

It was obvious that Miss Kitney didn't realise that the rock cakes had risen to double the size because Jessie had cleaned the range. On the other hand, this could be another case of balancing the books by making the cake mixture go further, but Jessie had resolved to stick to the rules.

In the evening, Mrs Williams had no sooner collected three suppers, than Miss Kitney brought them back to scrape half of the potatoes into the saucepan. Jessie was sure she had served the correct amount. 'I cooked fourteen pounds of potatoes and I've served them on to forty two plates.' She held out the iron saucepan. 'There are still a few portions left.'

'I still say you are giving them too much.'

'I thought it was three portions to a pound of potatoes.'

'Certainly not! It's two portions per pound.'

This statement convinced Jessie that she was inventing her own rules. She bit her lip and said, 'I'm sorry, I didn't know the Naafi had revised all the quantities.'

At Burscough, the latest memos were always clipped together and hung on the end of the dresser. When Miss Kitney departed with the suppers, Jessie searched the kitchen but couldn't find any of the circulars sent from Naafi headquarters.

During the next fortnight Jessie realised that Mrs Miles grumbles had been justified. As temporary cook, her day began at seven-thirty and finished at ten o'clock at night. The manageress hadn't offered any assistance or shown any appreciation, therefore Jessie was surprised when Gwennie said, 'Miss Kitney thinks you need a break. You haven't been out of the kitchen since you came. We can have a walk round Gravesend and perhaps you'd like to come and see my dad's shop.'

Jessie was about to wash the floor, but Gwennie insisted

There were quite a few customers in the boot shop, so they went for a brisk walk, but the wind was keen and they soon returned to the canteen. As they walked through the passage, the door of the coffee bar was ajar. Miss Kitney called, 'Jessie, would you come here a minute?'

In the bar, the manageress introduced Miss Hanna, the Area Supervisor, who said, 'I hear you've been helping out since cook left. You obviously enjoy cooking. Would you like to go to our training school in London? Of course your pay will increase when you are fully trained.'

The offer was so unexpected that Jessie didn't reply.

Miss Hanna continued, 'The next course will begin in six weeks' time. In the meantime, I'll transfer you to Eastchurch to work under Miss Wilson. She's an excellent cook.'

There was another pause.

'You would like to go to the training school wouldn't you?'

Jessie nodded.

'Your letter of introduction and instructions will be ready for you in the morning.'

In the kitchen Gwennie was waiting, eager to know what had transpired. When Jessie recounted the conversation she said, 'My friend, Daisy, was only there for a short time. She said it's the showplace of the area.'

'Well, if it's a showplace, at least it will be clean.'

'The Scottish manageress is a slave-driver.'

'I haven't spent my wages since I've been here. If I don't like it there, I can go home.'

'Why don't you go back and tell her you'd like to be nearer home?'

'Then the Naafi won't send me for the training.'

Gwennie looked at the clock. 'It's no use. I'll have to go.'

Jessie fetched the apple tart she had baked for the corporal's bar. 'Gwennie you'd better not let Miss Kitney see this. You've cut it into six and it's supposed to be divided into eight.'

'I haven't touched it, but my corporals will be pleased. They're going to be very sorry when they hear you've deserted them.'

Only three weeks after her arrival at Gravesend, Jessie was on her way to another canteen. As the train steamed through the Kent countryside, she surmised that the sealed envelope in her bag contained the letter from headquarters which cast doubt upon her honesty. Presumably, Miss Kitney had been instructed to keep her in the kitchen which was why she had called her a kitchen maid. It was now obvious that the manageress was annoyed because she had to serve in the coffee bar, while Jessie continued to receive the usual wage of a general assistant.

Miss Hanna would also have to obey instructions from headquarters, so she solved her staffing problem by transferring Jessie to another kitchen. The Naafi would then respond to an urgent request for a cook and trained general assistant.

Up to now, Jessie had aspired to becoming a charge hand because this was usually the next rung on the Naafi promotion ladder. She had been unaware that catering was a possible alternative. Now, the prospect of embarking on a new career filled her with optimism.

It was not until many years later that, with hindsight, Jessie was able to view the chain of events in perspective and realised that Providence had moved her on at that particular time: she was not destined to remain a general assistant all her life.

Appendix

£.s.d.

one guinea	=	twenty one shillings
one pound	=	twenty shillings
one shilling	=	twelve pennies (pence)
tuppence	=	two pence
one florin	=	two shillings
half a crown	=	two shillings and six pence

Abbreviations

C.O.	Commanding Officer
G.O.C.	General Officer Commanding
C.B.	Confined to barracks